HER FINEST HOUR

HER FINEST HOUR

ONE TEEN'S PERSONAL WAR WITH HITLER'S GERMANY

Stephen Doster

INTEGRATED MEDIA
NEW YORK

All rights reserved, including without limitation the right to reproduce this book or any portion thereof in any form or by any means, whether electronic or mechanical, now known or hereinafter invented, without the express written permission of the publisher.

Copyright © 2015 by Stephen Doster

ISBN: 978-1-5040-7822-1

This edition published in 2022 by Open Road Integrated Media, Inc.
180 Maiden Lane
New York, NY 10038
www.openroadmedia.com

INTRODUCTION

"General von Studnitz, who had served as German military attaché in Poland, said he appreciated it was the duty of the [U. S. military navel] attachés to gather intelligence for their government and he was quite willing to inform us fully and frankly. Von Studnitz gave the attachés a 'clear and concise summary of the military campaign to date' and predicted that 'mopping up operations in France would not require more than another ten days, after which preparations would begin for crossing the channel to England'. Von Studnitz believed the British, without a single army division intact and most of their heavy artillery abandoned at Dunkirk, would not resist. Hillenkoettner asked how the Germans would cross the Channel, but von Studnitz 'brushed aside this question with the comment that all plans were made. The war,' he added, 'would be over by the end of July, in six weeks.'"

> Charles Glass, *Americans in Paris: Life & Death Under Nazi Occupation*, London, Penguin Books, 2009, pp. 19–20.

What General von Studnitz and leaders of the Third Reich failed to realize—besides the fact that the English Channel precluded their

INTRODUCTION

effective use of blitzkrieg as a means of subduing enemy forces—was that Britain was a land of independent people, fiercely loyal to their queen, steadfast in the face of adversity, and fearless in war. These traits are exemplified by a sixteen-year-old teen named Marjorie Terry Smith who served on eight RAF stations. From her mid-teens to early-twenties, she lived in a perpetual state of war, never knowing when the next bomb might strike (her family was bombed out of three homes), losing her fiancée to Rommel's forces, and witnessing the horrors of warfare inflicted in friends, family, and the pilots of the RAF stations on which she served.

In recalling the past, she speaks of "before the war," "during the war," and "after the war," three distinct timeframes that define her life. As a result, this book is divided into three main sections. Citations throughout the text correlate to notes at the back of the book, which provide more information about the people and events she references.

The hubris of General von Studnitz might be forgiven when one considers that not only was Germany engaged in a futile effort to forge an empire, they were taking on a people who had actually built "an empire the sun never sets on", and, therefore, were not intimidated in the least by Herr Hitler and Co.

The British were protected by the Channel, an indomitable spirit, and Divine Providence. They also had two secret weapons. One was radar. The other was the average Brit, including one Ms. Marjorie Terry Smith.

HER FINEST HOUR

"... the Battle of France is over. I expect that the Battle of Britain is about to begin. Upon this battle depends the survival of Christian civilization. Upon it depends our own British life, and the long continuity of our institutions and our Empire. The whole fury and might of the enemy must very soon be turned on us. Hitler knows that he will have to break us in this island or lose the war. If we can stand up to him, all Europe may be freed and the life of the world may move forward into broad, sunlit uplands. But if we fail, then the whole world, including the United States, including all that we have known and cared for, will sink into the abyss of a new dark age made more sinister, and perhaps more protracted, by the lights of perverted science. Let us therefore brace ourselves to our duties, and so bear ourselves, that if the British Empire and its Commonwealth last for a thousand years, men will still say, *This was their finest hour*."

Winston Churchill's speech to the House of Commons of the Parliament of the United Kingdom on 18 June 1940

I. BEFORE THE WAR

Chapter One

TOOTING BEC, MERTON PARK, TERRY TERRY-SMITH

I'm Marjorie Catherine Terry Terry-Smith, although at the time I was born, I was only named Catherine Terry Smith. I was born on August the 13th, 1923 in the Florence Nightingale Nursing Home, Tooting Bec Common, South London. In the days of coach and horses when one went through a toll gate, one had to pay money and the man with the horn would blow on it to tell the toll gate keeper to come out to take their money. So it was called "Tooting."[1]

---

1 Tooting Bec is a place in the London Borough of Wandsworth in south London. It is named after Bec Abbey in Normandy, which was given land in this area (then part of the Streatham parish) after the Norman Conquest. Saint Anselm, the second Abbot of Bec, is reputed to have been a visitor to Tooting Bec long before he succeeded Lanfranc as Archbishop of Canterbury. Saint Anselm gives his name to the modern Roman Catholic Church which sits on the corner of Balham High Road and Tooting Bec Road. A relief sculpture of Saint Anselm visiting the Totinges tribe (from which Tooting as a whole gets its name) is visible on the exterior of Wandsworth Town Hall. Tooting Bec sits on Stane Street, a former Roman Road which linked Roman London with Chichester to the southwest. Tooting Bec appears in Domesday Book of 1086 as *Totinges*. It was held partly by St Mary de Bec-Hellouin Abbey and partly by Westminster Abbey. Its domesday assets were: 5 hides. It had 5½ ploughs, 13 acres (53,000 m^2). It rendered £7. The area includes Tooting Commons, which features Tooting Bec Lido, the largest fresh water pool in England as well as a small athletics stadium. Often considered part of Tooting, it forms the northern part of the latter suburb. Source: http://en.wikipedia.org/wiki/Tooting_Bec, accessed April 10, 2013.

My parents were born in the Victorian era in the 19th century. My father's family came from Lancashire where they had resided for some four or five hundred years. My mother's father's family came from France at the time of William the Conqueror when the name was spelled T-H-I-E-R-Y and was Anglicized after they came to England to T-E-R-R-Y. My mother's mother was Irish, although she was not born in Ireland. She was born in Greenwich, England. My father was an architect and surveyor. My mother had been brought up a Roman Catholic—very devout she was. I will tell you more about that later.

We lived in Merton Park, which was a new London subdivision with houses built between the two world wars. I remember my father saying how wonderful it was to be living only 19 miles from Piccadilly Circus, and here we were surrounded by countryside and farmland. It was wonderful until the London County Council decided that the land across the other side of the High Street, which was called Morden, was going to be developed and removed some of the slums from East London out here to the countryside. Then the London underground decided to extend to our area, so where we had farmland behind us, with cows mooing vaguely in the distance, we suddenly had trundling out from the bowels of the earth; the underground trains coming to the terminal. For some reason they called the terminal Morden, although it came out in Merton Park.[2]

---

[2] Merton Park is a place in the London Borough of Merton. It is a suburb situated between Wimbledon, Morden, South Wimbledon and Wimbledon Chase. It is 7.3 miles (11.7 km) south-west of Charing Cross. The area is part of the historic parish of Merton. . . . Until the last quarter of the 19th century, the parish of Merton was mainly rural. The area now known as Merton Park was farmland owned by City merchant John Innes who was the local "lord of the manor". The rapid development of Wimbledon to the north encouraged Innes to develop his land for housing. He took as his model the garden suburbs (particularly Bedford Park in Chiswick) and developed the tree-lined roads of detached and semi-detached houses for which the area is known. The northern section of Merton Park each side of Kingston Road is now a conservation area. The southern section, roughly from Circle Gardens southwards, was developed in the 1920s and 1930s, stimulated by the opening of the London Underground

So, we were soon surrounded by part of London and the noise of the underground. Merton Park was wrapped around an old village or little town called Merton. I went to Merton Park School, a little parochial school across the street from St. Mary's, a Saxon church where I was confirmed. To get to the school you went through an enclave of very old houses, and suddenly we were in another century. Back in the day, Lord Nelson and Lady Hamilton worshipped there because they lived in Merton. His hatchments were on the wall in his little pew. There was an unusual feature, what they called a spy hole, built into the church wall so people who were thought to be unclean or had a disease could take part in the service. They would be outside the church looking in and could see through to the altar area. I took confirmation classes in the rectory, which was a sort of a Georgian house or early Victorian next to the church. I would walk through a Sexton archway and have confirmation classes in the vicar's drawing room. After the war I worked at the BBC and was told by Heather Evans, who was also from Merton Park, that part of the church's roof had been damaged by a bomb.

The Reverend Dunk had been a wartime, World War I pilot. There was a propeller right over his mantel piece, the fire pit. I would go around daydreaming about Reverend Dunk. We nicknamed him Drunk, which was very unkind because he was a charming man. I could see him fighting the Red Baron in dramatic aerial fights. The confirmation class would be over and I hadn't heard a word they said. Somehow I managed to be confirmed by the Bishop of Guilford.

When I was about five years old, a neighbor asked my mother if I would go play with her son, John, in the garden because there had been a little girl playing with him and she was very rough

---

station at Morden. Housing here was developed on a smaller scale and is not as distinguished, nor is the area designated for conservation. Source: http://en.wikipedia.org/wiki/Merton_Park, accessed April 10, 2013

Terry with Uncle Herbert, her father's brother, WWI veteran.

and very rude, and she didn't want her there again. "But Marjorie is so sweet," that she knew I would get on with John, so I dutifully trotted around his house and went to the neighbor's entrance, which led to the garden, and played with him for about an hour. Then I went out to go home for lunch. When I came out of the gate and turned down the little part back to my house, there was this girl, this spurned girl, waiting with a brick in her hand. As I turned to walk away, she threw the brick at my back. I went flat on the ground. John called his mother who called my mother, and they both carried me back to Mother's house. The doctor came and said, "She must lie flat on her back for two weeks and not move." I don't know why they didn't take me to the Cottage Hospital, although I doubt that it boasted an X-ray machine in those days. Then a policeman came and took particulars from me, which upset me. Apparently this girl was a budding criminal.

Things were happening to me all the time it seemed. I had to have a tonsillectomy at the Nelson Cottage Hospital. All the children who were having tonsillectomies were seen at the same time. This very disagreeable nurse made us all line up and give us shots. The girl in front of me fainted and this nurse glared at me and said, "I suppose you're going to faint." I said, "No, I'm not." However much I felt like fainting I didn't. In those days you just walked into the operating room. I saw all these horrible sort of instruments beside the operating table that were going to go down my throat, and I decided I didn't want to have them done. I said to the surgeon, "Please, sir, my mother said it isn't really necessary for me to have my tonsils out." He said, "It's a bit late to think about that now." He said, "Let me look at your tonsils." He shined a torch into my throat and said, "You've got the worst, biggest tonsils of the lot. Get on that table." So I climbed on the table and they gave me an anesthetic which consisted of putting a mask over your face and dripping ether until you passed out. That night I woke up in the middle of the night with blood just gushing out of my mouth. I was quite frightened. I called for the nurse, not the same nurse, but another irritable nurse who came up and said, "What's the problem?" I said, "Well, I'm bleeding all over the place." She said, "Oh! All over this rubber mat!" All she did was turn the rubber pad over on the mattress, told me to climb back on the bed and not to make noise and wake anybody. I said, "Could I have a glass of water?" And she said, "No, you may not." So I was a very unhappy child until I went home after about four days. I had to have nothing but ice cream, and that made me feel quite a bit better.

Terry (right) and her sister, Sylvia.

Before I went to school, I was called Joy, which was derivative of Marjorie because I couldn't pronounce Marjorie very well. The reason I was called Marjorie was that my father had an aunt, which was his godmother, who lived on the outskirts of Paris. I never bothered to inquire as to whether she was actually French or she was married to a Frenchman or she was just living there. I don't know what the circumstances were, but my father was very fond of her. So as a compliment to her, he named me after her. Six months later, she died and left her home and estate to her housekeeper. The housekeeper's husband was to take care of the house and to look after all her cats. All I received out of it was a christening cup. But I stuck with the name Marjorie, which I was not very fond of, especially when it was shortened to Marge or Margie. I was named also Catherine which was a family name on my mother's side, and the Terry part is, of course, my mother's surname.

When I was quite young, my father had his office in London. His name was William Horace Smith. His initials were W. H. Smith, but in the same building, somebody else of the same name had his offices there. They were always getting each other's mail and each other's visitors. My father said, "This is ridiculous, and neither of us wants to move. I can't ask the other W. H. Smith to change his name. He has stationery shops all over the area we live in, if not all over England, and there are W. H. Smith kiosks on the main railway station." Eventually it became W. H. Smith & Sons.

So my father decided he better change his name—get it double-barreled. He was going to use his mother's maiden name, which was Gravatt and call himself Gravatt-Smith. My mother's brother, Uncle Charles, was killed in World War I. So she and my grandmother both pled with my father to add Terry in memory of Charles. Otherwise, the line would die out, so he changed his name to Terry-Smith; none of them thinking, of course, that then

I now became Marjorie Catherine Terry Terry-Smith, which was quite ridiculous, but nobody consulted me.

Charles Terry (front-right), World War I.

Before I went to school, I said I was called Joy, but my mother decided when I went to school I should be called Marjorie; my proper name. At that time, I had been sitting in on my sister's lessons because she was too frail to go to school. Sylvia had a French governess, so I think the poor woman babysat me while I listened to all of Sylvia's lessons. When mother took me to school for an interview with the headmistress, I told her I didn't really need to come to school because I knew everything. I thought by osmosis, I suppose, that I had absorbed all the lessons my sister had taken. Actually, the only thing I absorbed was the governess's French accent. The headmistress asked my mother why I had a French accent, and she explained that was all I had learned at these lessons. In reality, I really knew nothing. I was probably the worst student in that school since I daydreamed too much. That was my problem.

Thereafter, I was called Marjorie until I was about ten when I decided I wanted to be called Catherine. That didn't help because I was called Cat and Cathy, so eventually when I went to art school, I decided I wanted to be called Terry. I was called Terry from then on until right up to now.

Chapter Two

WWI VETS, SALVATION ARMY, CATHOLIC INFLUENCE, MRS. SOER

I was born five years after the end of World War I, but it had really no relevance to me at all. It could have been, you know, centuries ago, except it sort of just sunk into me eventually that when I would go shopping on the High Street with my mother, we would pass maybe four or five men walking in the gutter, holding out a cap for people to put money into; maybe one would play a banjo. One of them might be blind and would have his hand on the shoulder of the person in front of him to guide him along. I said to my mother, "Why are they doing this?" She said, "Because the government is not doing anything to help them when they come back from the war. They are wounded and can't work anymore." I thought this was dreadful.

Once near the underground station I saw a man standing with a placard on his chest that read, "I fought in World War I and I'm blind. Please help me." He held a little tray, which had boxes of matches on them. My father gave me sixpence and said, "Go and take it to that over to that man." I came back with a box of matches. My father said, "Take the box of matches back." I said, "Why? They only cost a penny to start with, and you gave him a sixpence. He said, "Because I will tell you later. Take it and put it back." So I put it back. My father explained to me, if the man was not selling something he would be moved on by the police for vagrancy or loitering. "This way he can legitimately stand there and get money from the public because that's his only way of keeping himself alive. But if everybody took one of his matches, then he wouldn't be able to do what he was doing."

There was a place in Richmond where wounded veterans would make poppies year round to sell on Poppy Day, on November the 11th. In those days on the 11th hour, the 11th day of the 11th month, all the traffic would stop and the local cannons would fire. There would be a two-minute silence, then after that a bugle would sound. In those days men wore hats, and they would take off their hats and everybody, traffic, everything would come to a standstill. That wouldn't be possible to do nowadays, but it was very moving at the time. I'm reminded every year of the people who have been killed in World War I.

Other results of World War I were that there were so many spinsters. Tens of thousands of soldiers were killed in one battle. There were very few young men left in England, so there weren't enough to go around. The whole time I was in school, there was only one elderly woman, at my first school I went to. Her name was Mrs. Messer. She was the only person I knew who was married. At my boarding school, there was one young teacher who was engaged. But apart from that, everybody else was a spinster. Every family I knew had spinsters. I had an aunt who never married as a result of not enough young men left in England to be married to; a very sad condition.

In World War I, my father was a cartographer stationed with the army in the Balkans. His two brothers were both in the army in France. Amazingly, they all came home intact, which was unusual in a family with three sons. My father was the last to come home. They were called the "Forgotten Army." All the other units would come home from Europe with lights blazing and bands playing. Then they finally remembered my father's outfit who came back quietly and sort of undercover almost. They were truly the forgotten army.

Wimbledon was the next town to us at Merton Park. One thing other children and I delighted in doing was walking up on Wimbledon Fortnight [tennis tournament] and getting tickets to see the players. My favorite thing was the intervals when they would have free teas, cream and strawberry teas. It was something to look forward to. Nowadays you have to book a ticket about a year beforehand as they have gotten so vast. It's like football games in the States, and just about as rowdy, too.

One thing I was unaware of as a child was the Depression. I didn't notice any difference in my lifestyle, but my parents and my father's parents all had their money in Farrow's Bank, which went under; left them with nothing. My father was an architect, but with the Depression there were very few people who could afford to have designer houses built. So my father became a surveyor and occasionally would design additions to houses or a sunroom or something like that that people wanted added onto their houses. He had to transfer his career. But I didn't notice any difference in my lifestyle as a child. So the Depression affected so many people, in so many ways, but my parents were very great in that it didn't seem to make any difference to our lives.

One of my father's colleagues was a very charming aristocratic man named Stanley Wood. He and his wife had no children, but he would invite our whole family over periodically to their very lovely house. Stanley had a game room, as he called it. He had designed and built a soccer table, a table with rows of soccer players.

Sylvia and I would play each other. My father asked him if he had patented his game, and he said he didn't intend to.

My mother once commented that she couldn't have had two daughters more different in temperament. Sylvia, the one who had a weak heart, was the most boisterous, enthusiastic, energetic and so easy to embrace new experiences. Then there was me; perfectly healthy but a very timid and shy child. Mother said that when Sylvia was about five years old, they went shopping. As they passed a cinema Sylvia said, "Oh, I hear music. What is that?" Mother said, "Come away, it's just a cinema. They have films, and I don't know what. Come away, darling." They went into a nearby department store. Mother was at the counter getting whatever she was ordering. When she finished, she turned around, and Sylvia was nowhere to be seen.

Frantically she ran out in the street, stopping people and saying, "Have you seen a little curly-haired five-year-old child anywhere?" She was running down the street and, as she neared the cinema, asked a woman the same question. A man standing by said, "I saw a small child going into that cinema, and I wondered how she was doing this by herself, but she was so small I didn't think the cashier at the window saw her." So Mother went into this cinema. Of course, it was dark, and at that point in those days they were silent films. They had no sound. They had a pianist who played appropriate music at appropriate times. Mother walked down the aisles looking for Sylvia and couldn't see her until she got to the bottom. Sylvia was happily sitting on a bench next to the woman playing the piano. Mother couldn't snatch her away without making a scene until the intermission came up. She went up to scold Sylvia, and the woman said, "Oh, she's definitely fine. She just sat happily by me and was just delighted with everything." Apparently Sylvia didn't miss Mother at all; she was so engrossed in this new thing.

Mother said, when I was about the same age, she had taken me to some department store. As she was at the counter making a purchase, I was fascinated with these overhead rails where the person behind the counter would put the money and the bill in a cylinder attached to one of these rails. It would go zooming along to the top of the room where there was a window with three women sitting there receiving all these cylinders, making the change and sending it back again. I took a couple of steps forward to see better as it was so interesting to me, and suddenly I looked and I couldn't see my mother anywhere. I started crying loudly and sobbing. Soon there was a crowd of people around me, including the floor manager. They were about to announce over the loud speaker about this missing child when my mother turned around from the counter, and said, "What's the matter?" I said, "You weren't there," and she said, "I was right behind you." That just shows Sylvia was so independent and I was so dependent.

The reason Mother was so shocked that Sylvia had gone into this cinema was because of her religious background. As I mentioned, she was a Catholic. Her family was Catholic. She was a *devout* Catholic and declared that she would become a nun when she was old enough. But she was coming back from mass with her grandmother one day when they passed a residential area where there was this circle of people. In the center was a girl who was reading from the Bible and, to Mother, this was so astounding because in the Catholic Church, they weren't allowed to read from the Bible or certainly not to own one. She couldn't believe that this was possible for anybody else. So she asked her grandmother who those people were, and the grandmother said, "Come away, that's that new ragtag group called the Salvation Army."

My mother was absolutely fascinated, so the next evening she made an excuse; she was going for a walk. She went to the Salvation Army hall and sat in the back. She was waiting for a bolt from heaven to hit her (because another brave thing for a Catholic to do was to go in any other sort of denominational church). To my Mother's astonishment, this person who was doing the service was a woman; this was unheard of. The woman took the service and gave the sermon. This was an eye-opener to my mother. She didn't know there was anything like that before for a woman to be able to do. At the end of the service, she said the Salvation officer came up to my mother and said, "I know that you haven't been here before. Why did you come today?" Mother said, "Because you can read the Bible here," then went on to explain that in the Catholic Church they weren't allowed to read the Bible. The Salvation officer gave my mother her own Bible, which my mother hid. About a year later she joined the Salvation Army. You can imagine how well that went down in Victorian times.

Of course, she was shunned from the family and everybody she knew, but she was determined. She went to seminary and became a Salvation Army officer. They have very strict rules. You are not allowed to wear any jewelry or makeup or go to any places of entertainment, be it the cinema or the theater, and you were not to make friends with the people where you were stationed because they thought this was not a good idea. Nor could you have any photos of your family. It was about as difficult as being a nun in a convent.

After my mother fell in love with my father, whose family was Anglican, she could no longer go on being an officer. You had to be an officer married to another officer to continue because they put the services together. So my mother brought us up with sort of both Catholic and Salvation Army mores, so to speak, so that we had a very strict upbringing. On Sundays we weren't allowed to listen to anything on the radio unless it was classical or religious music, and we weren't allowed to play games.

Years later I visited my sister who was living in Spain. She had a swimming pool, and she used to swim with her head held high out of the water. I said to her, "Sylvia, why do you swim like that?" She said, "Well, I can't bear to get water over my nose or my head." I said, "Neither can I. I wonder why that is." So when I went back to England and mentioned it to my mother, she said, "I may have an explanation for that. You know I was brought up in a Catholic school. When we bathed we weren't allowed to bathe in the nude; we had to wear a shift. I didn't like looking at naked bodies, even my own children, so when it was the nurses night off and I had to bathe you, I would wrap you in a towel and sort of dunk you in the water." I said, "Didn't my head go under?" She said, "Yes, quite frequently." So there was the answer, although how she got us clean just by dunking us in warm water, I don't know. There was the Catholic upbringing being visited on us.

When I was born, Sylvia was seven years old. She developed rheumatic fever, which left her with a weak heart. She had a weakened left ventricle and the doctor said she might live to her 21st birthday, if she didn't take part in any sports or do anything strenuous and rested every afternoon. This she totally ignored and lived to be—she was just two months shy of celebrating her 90th birthday; a life which she lived full tilt. Didn't listen to the doctors at all. She was very beautiful, talented *and* brilliant.

Mother had adopted in her social work a Hungarian woman we called Mrs. Soer (pronounced "sir" because no one could pronounce her real name) who was living in a nursing home run by the Red Cross about a mile away from us. Sylvia and I, every Sunday afternoon, had to walk to this nursing home and sit with this old lady who was paralyzed on one side. She was probably in her fifties, but she was old to us in this nursing home full of a lot of other old ladies. Apparently in Hungary her husband had been a very well-known, influential businessman. They were very wealthy until her husband's partner somehow made them bankrupt. Mrs. Soer's husband shot himself. The shock of it made her have a stroke, and so she was paralyzed in her bed. She said her servants came in and just calmly plundered her. Took her jewelry and went through her wardrobe, took her furs and all her clothes, and just kindly walked out and left her there. I guess the equivalent in Hungary of the Red Cross found her. During World War I they had a hospital in Belgrave Square London. It had given it over to the British Red Cross for homes for officers recuperating from their war wounds. She was sent to England under the aegis of the Red Cross. That's how we came to be looking after her. I felt very sorry for her, thinking of the life she had lived in Hungary compared to the way she was living then was really pathetic. Years later, I went to visit her. They couldn't afford to keep her anymore and had put her in a public ward in Kingston-On-Thames Hospital. When I went to visit her, she told the doctor that for years my sister and I had spent every Sunday visiting her; how she had become a Catholic and kept telling me how wonderful her Catholic friends had been to her.

Chapter Three

SUFFRAGETTES, BOARDING SCHOOL

An old school friend of my mother's was my godmother. I never knew what her first name was. Although she and my mother had been in school together, my mother always referred to her as Mrs. Mead. It was so formal in those days. Apparently her husband had a very good business in Bognor Regis in Sussex until the Depression. He lost his business, so they were living in a house in a suburb of London, which was reduced circumstances for them. They had a little maid named Edith that had come to them when she married. Edith was very frail person, but she had to do everything: cook the meals and clean the house. Every time I visited my godmother I'd stop by Edith's sitting room to say hello to her. She had one canary, but she had cages all around the room because every time a canary died, she'd have it stuffed and put in its cage. Then she'd buy another canary and a new cage. She had half a dozen in the room. I'd have to actually go around to find the live bird.

The Meads were very devout Methodists. On the landing of her second floor, she had one of those old pump organs that you pump with your feet. So I was playing about the only thing I could play on the organ which were music hall songs, like "Yes, We Have No Bananas," singing at the top of my voice. Suddenly a hand came on my shoulder. It was Mrs. Mead, and she said, "Marjorie, only religious songs are played on this organ." I was duly reprimanded.

Emmeline Pankhurst, who was the head of the suffragette movement in England, was also friend of Mrs. Mead. Suffragettes got so aggressive in their demands that some of them chained themselves to the railings of 10 Downing Street. On one occasion a woman [Emily Wilding Davison] at Epsom Derby, where the Kings Court was running, flung herself front of the horses and was trampled to death just to further the cause of suffragette movement. Mrs. Pankhurst apparently fled to my godmother's home and stayed with her while the police were looking for the head of the suffragettes to haul her off to jail. Somehow a newspaper reporter had found out where she was staying. One day they were sitting down to breakfast in the breakfast room when Edith came in to say that there was a newspaper reporter at the door. Mrs. Pankhurst was about to say tell them to go away, then she thought, *If he's found out about me, others will have found out, too, so I might as well give him my story.* So my godmother said, "Edith, go and light the fire in the parlor and tell him to wait in the hall. Then Mrs. Pankhurst will go in the parlor and he can come in to see her."

So Edith lit the fire, which was just taking off, and Mrs. Pankhurst went and sat down in the parlor. The reporter came in and they had their session. My godmother was appalled when she read the newspaper article that said, "Mrs. Pankhurst sat by a mean little fire." It made it sound as if she was living in a slum. My godmother was absolutely outraged that they referred to the poor surroundings in which Mrs. Pankhurst was living.[1]

---

[1] Emmeline Goulden was born on 14 July 1858 in Manchester into a family with a tradition of

Mrs. Pankhurst had a daughter named Sylvia, and I understand that is how my sister got her name.

Emmeline Pankhurst

My parents had some friends who were Salvation Army missionaries come to visit her with their two sons, William and Stewart. Sylvia, who was about 12 at the time, became so enthralled with these officers named Armstrong and their stories of their life in

---

radical politics. In 1879, she married Richard Pankhurst, a lawyer and supporter of the women's suffrage movement. He was the author of the Married Women's Property Acts of 1870 and 1882, which allowed women to keep earnings or property acquired before and after marriage. His death in 1898 was a great shock to Emmeline. In 1889, Emmeline founded the Women's Franchise League, which fought to allow married women to vote in local elections. In October 1903, she helped found the more militant Women's Social and Political Union (WSPU)—an organisation that gained much notoriety for its activities and whose members were the first to be christened 'suffragettes'. Emmeline's daughters Christabel and Sylvia were both active in the cause. British politicians, press and public were astonished by the demonstrations, window smashing, arson and hunger strikes of the suffragettes. In 1913, WSPU member Emily Davison was killed when she threw herself under the king's horse at the Derby as a protest at the government's continued failure to grant women the right to vote. Like many suffragettes, Emmeline was arrested on numerous occasions over the next few years and went on hunger strike herself, resulting in violent force-feeding. In 1913, in response to the wave of hunger strikes, the government passed what became known as the 'Cat and Mouse' Act. Hunger striking prisoners were released until they grew strong again, and then re-arrested. This period of militancy was ended abruptly on the outbreak of war in 1914, when Emmeline turned her energies to supporting the war effort. In 1918, the Representation of the People Act gave voting rights to women over 30. Emmeline died on 14 June 1928, shortly after women were granted equal voting rights with men (at 21). Source: http://www.bbc.co.uk/history/historic_figures/pankhurst_emmeline.shtml, accessed June 8, 2013

India that she became absolutely fascinated with anything to do with India. She got books from the library. My parents were really alarmed at her fanaticism about this country, India, which had caught her imagination. She grew up insisting that her future lay in India, and she was not going to rest until she got there. But she also became friends with William, who was the oldest; about a year or two older than her. He became like an older brother to me. I really thought he was getting to be a permanent fixture in our home.

His parents returned to England and were in a place, as per usual, in the poorest part of the town. They had very little money as Salvation Army people do, or don't. He had a brilliant mind, receiving scholarships to grammar school. Then he got a scholarship to Oxford and did brilliantly there. He was not very tall, but very slim; had blue eyes and fair hair. I loved him very much and so did Sylvia. He rowed for Oxford, which is a grueling race; the Oxford and Cambridge race, which captures our country's imagination. It used to be that everyone wore favors on their coats; light blue for Cambridge and dark blue for Oxford. There's an area in the Thames where you're pulling against the tide, I suppose; really grueling. It left William with a weak heart as a consequence of the strain of pulling and fighting the current there. When he came down from Oxford with a degree and went to work for the foreign office, he decided he would not be going to make enough money to ask Sylvia to marry him. So she said she was very fond of him as a brother. That was a big disappointment to both families because they always sort of had holidays together, and we thought we were a permanently bonded family. He went on to become a member of the cabinet and then ended up being Lord Armstrong. So Sylvia could have been Lady Armstrong, but I don't think that came in to her thinking at all.

When I was about 10 or 11, my parents decided to send me to a boarding school. It was a Catholic boarding school with a lay teacher. It was a rather strange school in that it was very old-fashioned, in one way. In another way, it was very advanced in that before the war, as a whole, girls didn't dream of going to university. There were only two universities as far as I know for women: one in Oxford and one in Cambridge. I always thought women who went to university were rather strange people. They were called blue stockings for some reason. But Ms. Darling, who was the headmistress of the school, had quite a brilliant degree from Cambridge. She would float around in her gown being impressive. The brighter students were coached for sitting for Cambridge entrance. I was not one of them, obviously. The old-fashioned part was that we had lessons in deportment, etiquette and ballroom dancing, but also we had Swedish gyms, field hockey and lacrosse in the winter; tennis and swimming in the summer. The Swedish gym was my nightmare because the summer before I went to Beaulah House, I had fractured my elbow falling off a horse. Naturally, I didn't fall off it. I was flung off it. Somebody had put the saddle on for me. It had slipped around while I was going across a plowed field—just threw me off balance onto the field, and I broke my arm.

Terry Smith on horseback, Rustington, Sussex, 1938.

So when I went to school, I had a chit from my doctor to say that I wasn't to take part in my any strenuous physical activities until my arm healed. I had this sort of like a prison warden gym teacher who said, "Oh, nonsense, these exercises will strengthen your arm," (because she knew much better than the doctors). We had exercises, like sloth walking, which was a bar across the top of the ceiling we had to crawl along, leaping over a horse, parallel bars, and bars which were attached to a wall where you hung upside down. Of course my arm wouldn't support my weight and gave way. I hit my head on the ground and passed out. I think I was proving the gym teacher wrong as she was very annoyed about it saying, "You're doing this deliberately just so that you wouldn't have to do any more gym."

I was really hopeless in school when it came to academics. The only thing I enjoyed was history and art. The thing was that beforehand I had gone to this little parochial school and I realized that this school was about a year or two years ahead of the curriculum to my old school. There were only about ten girls in each class. I was very shy and afraid to keep on putting up my hand saying, "Please, I don't understand," because it was all Greek to me. I just let it go. I just made wild stabs at French and English grammar, declensions and things like that I never heard of. I was particularly hopeless at Math, so when I was 13—school-leaving age was 14 in those days—we had speech day. My parents came and Ms. Dolly took them aside and said, "I don't think academics lay in Marjorie's future, but she has been taking extra classes for art in which she really is very good. So I might suggest that she should go on to art school and not continue on here." That solved a problem for all of us. The school would no longer be tied down to this hopeless, non-academic student, and my parents wouldn't have to pay school fees anymore.

I don't know how I had the nerve to do this, but I used to go to mistress and say, "My parents would really prefer me to take extra art classes" instead of whatever was not the favorite class with me. The only class I didn't skip was Math because I thought my parents wouldn't buy that at all nor the headmistress. They were so indifferent to my academic achievements that they said, "Oh, go ahead." So when my parents were apprised of this news they told me, "Yes, all right, you can go to Wimbledon College of Art, but you will have to go to evening classes and take all the subjects that you missed by taking extra art classes." I thought I was being so clever, sort of bucking the system so to speak, and found out you can't do that really. So there I was starting art classes, which had homework, of course, and then in addition, I was going to evening classes and having homework there. I was really burdened. Weekends were spent with just trying to catch up with everything.

Terry Smith in her teens.

We just experienced the wedding of William and Kate. When they came out on the balcony and had that kiss, it reminded me of years ago when I was six or seven. King George V and Queen Mary were celebrating their 25 years on the throne or celebrating something like that, and my father, my mother, my sister and I went down early along Pall Mall before the rush of people came. We got quite near to the palace gates when my mother fainted.

The emergency care area was up on this big ornate memorial to Prince Albert, I think, in front of the palace. Father, Sylvia and I were trying to push against the crowd to get back to this place. Somehow I guess I had Sylvia's hand. She let go or I let go and suddenly here I was alone. All I could see were legs and tall people; all pushing against me to get to the palace, and I was trying to push against them to get to Mother. I said, "My mother is up there on the memorial. She's fainted and I can't get to her." So they passed me over their heads until I got to the bottom of the memorial. I went up to my father and sister who were anxiously watching my mother as this Boy Scout squeezed a big sponge over mother's face and brought her to, which was a rather drastic thing to do. She sat up and said, "Little boy, you have ruined my hat."

She had bought a new cloche hat for the occasion. She was more concerned about that. I suddenly realized we had a wonderful view above the crowds; a clear view of the palace balcony. So we really thanked Mother in the end for fainting because we could stand up there; not being pushed out by the crowd. We saw the king and queen come out on the balcony. That was a memorable occasion on top of the memorial.

Chapter Four

LAURENCE OLIVIER, HOUSEMAIDS, CORNISH RIVIERA, HITLER, UNDERGROUND TRAIN CRASH

One of the advantages in living where we did in Merton, being able to get on the underground and be up in central London in no time at all, was that we could go up to see shows, opera, ballet and concerts. Once I went with Sylvia to the Old Vic where they were doing Shakespeare. Laurence Olivier was Hamlet; we were about two rows back from the front. I had only seen Hamlet done by us in school, with very limited acting there, so I wasn't prepared for the emotions that were shown by these actors. At one stage in the play, Hamlet sees his ghost. He, Laurence Olivier, dropped to the floor and gagged. His head was hung over the edge of the stage; sort of gasping and clutching his throat. All of a sudden I thought it was very funny, so I started laughing. Of course, it was such an intense moment in that scene that there was dead silence. Sylvia gradually moved further and further away from me, trying to pretend she had never seen this wretched child before. But, of course, the more she told me to shush, the more hysterical I got. She never took me to the Old Vic again.

We had a series of housemaids before the war. One of them particularly I didn't like. Her name was Joan, from Wales. She was an awful liar. My mother couldn't believe there were any grown-ups in the world that would lie. But Joan used to break things and then tell Mother that Ms. Marjorie did it. Mother would berate me and I would say, "I didn't." She would berate me more because was I saying that Joan was a liar. I wasn't very comfortable around Joan. I tried to stay away from her; to be at the other end of the house if she broke something, so that Mother knew it wasn't me. Mother used to also insist that I help Joan with the washing, but I used to wait until she got done to the last dish and say, "Can I help you, Joan?" She would say, "It's too late now." I remember once my parents went away for the weekend, but before they went away my mother had gone to a rather exclusive boutique and bought a model suit. She wasn't going to wear it because they were going to the country, so she just hung it in her wardrobe. When she came back a few days later, she went to some affair wearing this suit. Her neighbor said, "Oh, what a lovely suit. It reminds me of while you were away I saw your maid going down the street wearing a suit very similar." My mother said, "There is no way she could be wearing another suit. This is a model. This is the only one." So when she got home she tackled Joan who said, "Well, you just left it hanging in the wardrobe. You hadn't even worn it yet." That, thankfully, was the end of Joan.

We had another maid, Elsie. Very sweet girl, but she got TB somehow; probably had it when she came to us. She had to go into a recuperation place where they took TB patients. She had a very pretty round face. She was enamored of some silent film star. She had just shaved her eyebrows; put pencil marks there where her eyebrows would be but higher up. She appeared constantly as if she was surprised at something. It was as much as you could do to see her and not sort of laugh as she looked something comical. Bless her heart.

Mother had found a place in London called Gallery Lafayette, a French store. She bought me several dresses, different from English schoolgirl clothes, of which I was delighted. Of course, we wore uniforms at school, but when I was at home I just liked these dresses. They were all so different. She also went on another floor and found they sold servants clothes. She bought a whole lot of clothes for whoever our current maid was. It was the envy of the others maids in the area because she had these frilly caps and hats; one dress for morning and one for the afternoon. Our maids were the envy of the neighborhood.

Up until about the age of ten, we always used to spend our summer holidays down what we laughingly called the Cornish Riviera. Not quite so warm as the south of France Riviera, but it's lovely countryside. We loved Cornwell and Devon. That's the two places we used to go when I was young. Then, for some inexplicable reason, my father suddenly decided one summer that we would go to the Grand Hotel in Norfolk, which was on the east coast, not half as warm as the south coast. I think I mentioned I don't like the water, so what possessed me one early morning to get up before my family and put on my swim suit I don't know. I put it down to the Irish ancestry in me, which sort of bursts forth occasionally and makes me do crazy things. I look back on it in astonishment. I took my rubber floater ring with me and went down to the private beach. It was lovely for Norfolk, a warm day, so I glided into the water, then laid back and just floated. It was beautiful. I was just floating along, when suddenly I sort of sat up. To my horror I realized that the tide was going out and that the Grand Hotel was like a small toy building in the distance. I was panic stricken because I swam very poorly; I knew I couldn't fight the tide. There was this one person on the beach I could see in the distance. I yelled and waved my arms. It turned out to be a young man about 18 and an excellent swimmer. He raced out, caught hold of my ring and said, "Hang on." He dragged me back to the shore. I was really shaking; so frightened. He gave me a stern lecture for an 18-year-old about swimming by myself and not to ever do this again. I promised him I wouldn't, but said, "Please, if you meet my parents, don't tell them what I did." So he promised. I crept back into my room, had a warm bath and hid my swimsuit so no one would be suspicious.

There were three things I remember about the Grand Hotel. Mother was less than inspired about the menu, especially their soup. No one, the whole time we were there, ever offered us more than two soups. One was brown Windsor soup and the other was consommé. That was all that was offered in the way of soup. Mother said, "They are the cheapest soups to make. You just need some beef cubes put in a pot of water; one of them being consommé. You added some corn starch to the other and that would be your Windsor brown soup." The first time we went there, the waiter would say, "Brown Windsor soup or consommé." The second season we were there he just referred to them as "thick" or "thin," so from then on soup was referred to as either thick or thin. On the way to the dining room, one went past the entertainment center, the billiard room, the table tennis room and on the side of the corridor there was a row of One-Armed Bandit slot machines. One day, just for fun, I pulled down the lever. To my astonishment, a flood of money came out. I had to hold out my skirt for money to fall into. People coming towards the dining room stopped for this phenomenon, oohing-and-aahing. Then my parents came along, who were horrified because they didn't believe in gambling. They said, "We must take this to the manager at once and give it back to him." I said, "Why? The money was just sitting there, and I discovered it." "It's tainted money," according to Mother, so sadly I had to relinquish it to the manager. I felt very miffed about that.

The hotel also had a long bowling court. Mother got to talking with this man who was chatting her up about bowling. She said, "I'm not familiar with lawn bowling." He said very condescendingly, "Oh, I'm a champion. If you like, I will teach you." So he gave my mother a few pointers. Every week they would have a tournament, and Mother beat him at bowling. I never saw anybody look more furious than this champion who had been beaten by a beginner. But Mother got so enthused that afterwards when we came home she bought a set of bowling balls. There was a place near us that had a bowling lawn, and Mother got a beautiful white outfit. If you bowled, men had to wear white suits, slacks and shirts, and the women similar skirts. So Mother really enjoyed bowling. She became very proficient at it.

Then Mother decided to buy a little place near Worthing, Sussex, so we used to go down there on summer weekends. The summer I turned fourteen we went to France, Belgium and then Holland. The place we stayed in Belgium was off the main High Street. You went through an archway where there was this sort of square in front of the hotel, which had originally been a monastery. It had been occupied by the Germans in World War I as their headquarters in Bruges. The manager invited me into his study one day and showed me this German helmet with this spike on the top, a lethal looking thing, and other memorabilia he had left over from the German occupation. He referred to a German bitterly as a Bosch. Little did he know that only a few years later, they were going to overrun Belgium again. When we went into Holland, I had gotten rather fascinated with this new German regime, this Adolf Hitler who had come into power. I begged my father, "Couldn't we just go over into Germany just to see what's going on?" My father said, "I don't want to have anything to do with Germans or Germany," due to his experience in World War I, so we never did go there.

This was about the time I was fourteen and Sylvia was twenty-one. She was well into her journalistic career, working on Fleet Street on the oldest woman's magazine called *Horner's Stories*. She and the editor, Evelyn Aspinall, got along well. Evelyn was a very tall woman who never married. She moved to South America when she retired. Sylvia always went on the underground from Merton to Fleet Street. One day Sylvia was going to work on the underground train, which had stopped to let another train go by, but apparently the signal hadn't been working behind the train. Another train coming around the corner ran right in the back of it, pushing the last carriage in the front train and the first carriage in the second train right into the roof. Sylvia was in the last carriage in the first train. She said people were killed by the impact and the flying glass. She said "I had to run downhill to get to the doors."

Ultimately, some men were there that survived and could pull the doors open; they were automatic doors and were controlled remotely. She said she managed to get out and they had to walk along the tunnel with flames coming from the train, which was quite terrifying. That's when she realized that Evelyn Aspinall was in the first carriage of the second train. She trailed behind her and they walked along the tunnel in the dark until they came to the next station where they were helped up onto the platform. When Sylvia came home that evening, Mother said, "Did you read in the evening news about that terrible train accident. So many people killed!" I think it was the first train accident that happened since we had this underground train. Sylvia said, "Yes, I know, it must have been awful." She took me aside afterwards and said the usual, "Don't tell the parents, but I was on the first train." Why with her heart condition she didn't have a heart attack right there and then in the train, I don't know. She amazingly survived more events like that.[1]

---

[1] The Charing Cross (District Line) tube crash occurred on 17 May 1938 at about 09:55 hours, between Charing Cross (now Embankment) and Temple stations. Six people were killed when a Circle Line service ran through a false clear signal into the rear of a District Line service held at an automatic signal. The track circuits connected to the signal cabin at Charing Cross had been converted to alternating current on the morning of 8 May. As a result, there was some wiring which needed to be secured. This work was carried out during the engineering hours on 17 May. The signal wiring engineer had secured and reconnected all wires between the various circuit breakers in the cabin. However, one wire, which linked circuit breaker number 8 to circuit breaker number 9 had been put on the wrong terminal of circuit breaker number 9, thereby causing signal EH9, the eastbound starter signal, to clear too soon, with a train held at automatic signal number 823. The cabin was put into automatic mode as this was how it was normally set, but no testing was carried out, and traffic began with no observation from the engineers. Manual working was only used when a train was to be reversed at Charing Cross. The problem was first noticed as the line became busy, and was reported by a motorman on arrival at Temple, at 09:40. The motorman reported that he had nearly run into the train ahead. The message was conveyed to Charing Cross but no prompt action was taken despite further reports that the signal was clearing too soon. By the time it became clear that there was a significant problem, it was too late to prevent the collision. The report to the Ministry of Transport held the Signal Installer and Chief Lineman responsible for the wiring error and the failure to test the signals thoroughly, and the Station Foreman, Porter and Inspector responsible for not acting promptly to prevent a collision. A similar accident involving a signal wiring error had occurred near the same station on the Northern Line on 10 March. Source: http://en.wikipedia.org/wiki/Charing_Cross_(District_Line)_tube_crash, accessed April 15, 2013.

Chapter Five

WIMBLEDON ART SCHOOL, MURDERER, ADMIRAL DOMVILLE, IRA BOMBINGS, MEALS ON WHEELS

When I first attended Wimbledon Art School, it was on the top floor of the technical college. We didn't have a lot of room, and I thought at first I was going to straightaway start painting. But first I had to learn perspective, then we had to draw some very dusty and rather moth-eaten animals that were in glass cases. I think they were from the Victorian era and were sort of molted when you took them out to draw. We had to learn to create different textures. We also had to sort of draw silk to get to know that. Well, fortunately at Beulah House, I had a very good art mistress who had made use do that sort of thing. She had her tweed coat over the door and asked us to get the folds, the way the folds fall and also the texture. I thought it very easy to draw the tweed texture. I was the only one in the class who could. I thought all you have to do is look at it and draw it. I couldn't see the difficulty, but that first year we were honing our skills, I suppose; deciding what route we wanted to go.

I thought I'd follow my father and be an architect. I designed some lovely buildings until the art master would say, "That's very fine, but where do you put the power points and what about the plumbing system?" I said, "Oh, if I have to think about all that, I will do something else." I decided to go into theatrical design—much more exciting and much less constricting, so I thought.

I enrolled at the art school in Wimbledon, which was part of a technical college. It was located in a residential area. Part of the new school they built was on the site of a house my Aunt Edith had lived in. When I was young I would play in her garden, and when I was in art school, I would often sit in what used to be my aunt's garden. Next door to Aunt Edith's house lived a nice looking young man about six or seven year older than I. When I was a little girl, we used to play together. I forgot what his Christian name was, but his surname was Heath. When I had been there about 18 months, the Wimbledon County Council decided that we should move to our own school separate from the technical college, which was great. The new art school was about three or four miles away from where I lived. I'd walk across a park for a shortcut and come out into the road where the art school was. By the time I was at art school that young man I had known had apparently become an RAF officer. He had gone to stay at one of the many holiday camps springing up around Britain, had gotten to know some girl and murdered her.

One day there were several policemen up and down the road. One of them stopped me and said, "Where were you going?" which I thought was pretty obvious because I had a portfolio under my arm. I said, "I'm going to the art school. What's the problem?" He said, "Well, there is an escaped prisoner. We have a nationwide warning out that he might be anywhere, but actually we think he may be coming home to see his family, so we're patrolling to make sure. If he does decide to come, we will catch him." I thought, *Well, gosh, I think he's going to be slightly deterred if he was trying to get home to see his parents and sees the street full of police. Wouldn't that give him a warning?* Then I realized, *Oh, my gosh that was the little boy I used to play with in the garden years ago.* Back in those days, at the start of the war there was so little serious crime in England that this crime made headlines in the newspapers. They even made a movie about it. I thought it was extraordinary that this young boy and I used to play in the garden at my aunt's, and here he was escaping from the police. Of course, they got him in the end and the old chap was hanged.

I made some good friends at the art school, especially one Miranda Domville. In fact, we had decided that we were going to open a business on Bond Street, one of the most exclusive streets in London in those days. We were going to design and sell dresses and also supply costumes for plays and theaters in general. Where the money was coming from, we didn't know. How one has such lofty ideas when one is young! Miranda's father was a retired admiral. They were a very nice family and lived on Wimbledon Common. He thought the reason that Germany and Britain were at such odds with each other was that they didn't understand each other's characteristics or nationality enough. So, he set up a scheme called "The Link" whereby German and British college students would exchange visits and live with each other's families.

Apparently this was a wonderful idea for a while, until the British Secret Service became aware that Hitler was sending spies over, or anyway it was rumored that that was what was happening. So Admiral Domville at the beginning of the war was imprisoned in his house for the total of the war as a sort of enemy of the country, which broke his heart because he had just been such a faithful and loyal sailor for his country. It seemed very odd to me that his son, Barry, who was an army officer, was allowed to be in the British army if his father was suspected of being, a spy. Barry was killed in World War II.[1]

About 1938 there was an amazing amount of terrorist activity. The IRA [Irish Republican Army] was planting bombs in public places; everybody had gotten the jitters about them. One day I arranged with Miranda to meet her in Putney. We were going to lunch and then we were going to see a movie. She said, "We're going to meet Compton," (her other brother), "at the cinema." So we tromped along to the cinema and met him. We were sitting

---

[1] Admiral Sir Barry Edward Domvile KBE CB CMG (1878–1971) was a distinguished Royal Navy officer who turned into a leading British Pro-German anti-Semite in the years before the Second World War. Domvile was the son of Admiral Sir Compton Domvile and followed his father into the Royal Navy. Before the First World War he was Assistant Secretary to the Committee of Imperial Defence, and during the war he commanded destroyers and cruisers in the Harwich Force. After the war he became Director of Plans, and Chief of Staff to the Commander-in-Chief, Mediterranean before becoming, in 1925, commanding officer of the battleship *Royal Sovereign*. He became director of the Department of Naval Intelligence from 1927 to 1930, then commanded the Third Cruiser Squadron from 1931 until 1932, and served as President of the Royal Naval College, Greenwich from 1932 to 1934. Domvile had already visited Germany in 1935, being impressed by many aspects of the Nazi government, and was invited to attend the Nuremberg Rally of September 1936 as a guest of the German Ambassador Joachim von Ribbentrop. He became a council member of the Anglo-German Fellowship, and founded the Anglo-German organization, The Link. He supported St. John Philby, the anti-semitic British Peoples Party candidate in the Hythe by-election of 1939 and visited Salzburg that summer, attracting some criticism. In June 1940 his mistress, Mrs. Olive Baker, was arrested for distributing leaflets in favor of the Nazi radio broadcasts to Britain. She tried to commit suicide in prison, and was sentenced to five years imprisonment. Due to his pro-Nazi views, Domvile was interned during World War II under Defence Regulation 18B from 7 July 1940 to 29 July 1943. His experience in internment increased his anti-Semitism and led him to develop a conspiracy theory about an organization he called 'Judmas' ("the Judaeo-Masonic combination, which has wielded such a baneful influence in world history"). Domvile was a prolific diarist. When internment was imminent he hid the latest (56th) volume of his diaries in his garden where it was not discovered by the authorities. Admiral Domvile's pro-Nazi and anti-Anglo-German war sympathies were blatantly expressed in an endorsement to the 1939 book *The Case for Germany*. His endorsement consisted of the comment in the preface: "It is a great pleasure to me to introduce the public to Dr. Laurie's valuable book on modern Germany. He is best known to the world as a brilliant scientist, but he has found time in the intervals of his work to pursue with ardor the task upon which every sensible member of the British and German races should be engaged—namely the establishment of good relations and a better understanding between these two great nations.

up in the balcony, and halfway through the A movie I suddenly became aware of a ticking noise. I thought, *My gosh, could that be an IRA bomb?* I don't know where my mind was. It wasn't anywhere obviously because I decided not to say anything until the intermission. I didn't want to spoil the film for people. It was immaterial that we would all be blown up. At intermission the lights went up, and I said to Miranda, "Miranda, do you hear a ticking noise?" She said, "Oh, my gosh, yes, I do." She turned to Compton who said, "Yes, I heard a ticking noise." She said, "Do you think it could be an IRA bomb?" He said, "I doubt it. It's my alarm clock I just bought." Apparently Compton, in reaction to the government's attitude to his father, had become a conscientious objector, but, of course, he had to do something, so he was going to work on the land. He bought the alarm clock. I was such a clod.

One time I did keep a diary with dates in it. The diary is long since lost. I can't remember whether it was towards the end of '38 or the beginning of 1939 that we became aware that war was inevitable. From 1937 onwards we had been receiving hundreds and hundreds of refugees from the low-countries, mostly Jewish. My mother had become an organizer for the WVS (Women's Voluntary Service) started by Lady Reading.[2]

Dr. Laurie knows full well that this friendship is the keystone to peace in Europe—nay, in the whole world. He is one of the small group who founded the Association known as The Link, whose sole aim is to get Britons and Germans to know and understand one another better. He is one of the most zealous workers in this good cause in the country. He writes of the National Socialist movement with knowledge and great sympathy. The particular value of this book lies in the fact that it is written by a foreigner, who cannot be accused of patriotic excess in his interpretation of the great work done by Herr Hitler and his associates. I recommend this volume with confidence to all people who are genuinely impressed with the desire to understand one of the greatest—and most bloodless—revolutions in history." Admiral Sir Barry Domvile 8th May 1939. Source: http://en.wikipedia.org/wiki/Barry_Domvile, accessed June 8, 2013

2 The WRVS (formerly the Women's Voluntary Service, known until 1966 as the Women's Royal Voluntary Service) is a voluntary organization concerned with helping people in need throughout England, Scotland and Wales. It was founded as the Women's Voluntary Service in 1938 by Stella Isaacs, Marchioness of Reading as a British women's organization to aid

Mother was in charge of two districts, Merton Park and Morden, and had a coterie of ladies, volunteer ladies, who wore becoming little green pork pie hats, green tweed suits and maroon and white-striped blouses; very smart, as far as uniforms can look smart. They set up shop literally in an empty store in the High Street of Morton. I was called upon to, when I came home from school, go and run errands and make tea for them. I remember Mother was very agitated with all these refugees coming in.

Each district was given so many refugees that they had to find housing for, so my mother went to the Merton County Council Board of Directors and told them her requirement; that she needed a building with so many cots in it with washing apparatuses and also a place for them to eat meals. The Board sat around looking at each other and said, "Well, Mrs. Terry-Smith, we will take these into abeyance. We will let you know at the next meeting," (which would be in a month's time). My mother rapped the table and said, "I wanted this yesterday, but I will settle for it tomorrow!" She said they had a shocked look on their faces since they had never, ever been asked to produce something within a week, much less a day. My mother said, "These refugees are here, here and now. They need sustenance, somewhere to rest their heads and it's up to you to provide this facility for me!"

By George, they pulled themselves together and did supply a building where Mother could carry out this plan of hers. My father designed it for seating arrangements and decided it should

---

civilians. On 16 May 1938, the British government set out the objectives of the Women's Voluntary Service for Civil Defense: It was seen "as the enrolment of women for Air Raid Precaution Services of Local Authorities, to help to bring home to every household what air attack may mean, and to make known to every household [in the country] what it can do to protect itself and the community." In the words of the then Home Secretary, Sir Samuel Hoare, "as regards their civil defense functions, the Minister regards the Women's Voluntary Service as occupying . . . much the same relationship as that of the women's auxiliary services for the armed forces of the Crown." Source: http://en.wikipedia.org/wiki/WRVS, accessed April 16, 2013

be run on sort of army canteen lines where they had a buffet to take their own food to the table, which would therefore cut out a lot of help. Mother was in her element then. Everybody in the country was required to fill in a form stating the number of people in their house and occupations, et cetera. Mother was alarmed to find out how many people in her district lived alone and had no means of support; many of them were unable to go and get news themselves. So she started with these ladies. When they made themselves a casserole, they made another casserole, then they would take it to these shut-ins.

My father said, "This is an organization you've started, what do you want to call it?" Mother said, "I don't know." My father suggested Meals on Wheels, which, of course, that's what it became. They thought it was such a good idea—it must be the same in other districts—that my mother sent this information to headquarters to Lady Reading. Lady Reading's secretary wrote to say how much Lady Reading appreciated the information, and to mother's amazement, a few days later in the paper she read that Lady Reading was inspired to assist those who were shut-ins *and* to start an organization which will be called Meals on Wheels. No mention of Mother. Lady Reading's secretary wrote to Mother and said, "I'm so sorry you're not getting any recognition, but that's Lady Reading; any new ideas that come her way become her ideas." Mother said, "I don't mind. I am not looking for medals or awards. I'm doing something which needs to be done."[3]

---

[3] Meals on Wheels are programs that deliver meals to individuals at home who are unable to purchase or prepare their own meals. The name is often used generically to refer to home-delivered meals programs, not all of which are actually named "Meals on Wheels." Because they are housebound, many of the recipients are the elderly, and many of the volunteers are also elderly but able-bodied and able to drive wheeled vehicles, usually a van. Meals on Wheels originated in Great Britain during the Blitz, when many people lost their homes and therefore the ability to cook their own food. The Women's Volunteer Service for Civil Defense (WVS, later WRVS) provided food for these people. The name "Meals on Wheels" derived from the

WVS's related activity of bringing meals to servicemen. The concept of delivering meals to those unable to prepare their own evolved into the modern programs that deliver mostly to the housebound elderly for free or with donations. The first home delivery of a meal on wheels following World War II was made by the WVS in Hemel Hempstead, Hertfordshire, England in 1943. Many early services used old prams to transport the meals, using straw bales, and even old felt hats, to keep the meals warm in transit. This type of service requires many volunteers with an adequate knowledge of basic cooking to prepare the meals by a set time each day. The majority of local authorities have now moved away from freshly cooked food delivery, and towards the supply of frozen pre-cooked re-heatable meals. Source: http://en.wikipedia.org/wiki/Meals_on_Wheels, accessed April 16, 2013

II. WAR

Chapter Six

WORTHING, WAR DECLARED, MESSERSCHMITT PILOT, WVS, THE PHONEY WAR

My father bought a weekend house down on the coast between Worthing and Shoreham. We made friends with a family named Richards who had two sons, Peter and John, and a daughter. They were the mainstay of the local theatrical scene and were always putting on plays. Occasionally there were mishaps on stage. In one play, Peter was banging on a door saying, "Let me in! Let me in!" Well, the door opened by itself! He had to pull it shut again and go on banging away on it.

Once we were at our house down on the south coast at Lancing about 1936 or '37 and decided to go for a walk on the beach. We had only arrived the day before. We passed a neighbor who was working in the garden, his daughter was leaning out of the window talking to him and they both started talking to us. My mother could hear the radio in the room behind the daughter and said, "Oh, any news?" The daughter put her head back and said, "Oh, yes, well, war is being declared," in a very offhand way. So we sort of digested this and then wended our way down to the beach. We had only been there a few minutes when one of the officious neighbors came along. He had become an air raid warning warden; carrying his gas mask. He said, "Get off the beach at once. Don't you know war is being declared?" My father sort of shaded his eyes and looked out and he said, "I believe I see a speck in the distance. Could that be the invasion starting?" This chap was terribly annoyed that Father was, as the cockneys say, taking a Mickey out of him, sort of pointed back to where we lived and said, "Go home at once!" We said, "Yes, sir," and sort of tucked our forelocks and went back. It was so ridiculous.

Just before you got to the beach, there was a big pond. They called it the lagoon, and across the lagoon was a little footbridge. The authorities took two planks out of the middle of the footbridge, so that when the Germans landed they wouldn't be able to get across the footbridge. Well, for goodness sake, the lagoon at deepest was only about waist high. Do you think the Germans were going to line up to go across the bridge anyway? Well, we all thought it was towards the war effort.

1940 Surbiton, Surrey air raid wardens. Horace Smith, Terry's father, under the "X."

Another time, when I was in Lancing after the war began, I had gone into Shoreham to do some shopping and was coming back on the Old Salts Farm Road. This road was near an airfield. I used to lean over the wall and look at the Tiger Moths. I was dying to fly back then! I was walking next to a cornfield that had already been harvested and saw a Messerschmitt that had crashed landed. There was a railway embankment separating the cornfield from a private airfield that was either then or would later be the air-sea rescue airfield attached to Tangmere. The pilot had run out of petrol and was trying to land on the airstrip. A farmer had come out of his house and was holding the pilot at gunpoint until the authorities arrived. Meanwhile, he took the pilot's boots and gave this young German a cigarette. When I got there, the pilot was sitting on one of the wings, bootless and smoking this cigarette. People were on the roadside waving at him, and he waved back. I thought, *What a crazy war this is.*

Old Salts Farm Road (bottom-right), railway embankment (diagonal), airfield (top-right).

During the war nobody was allowed to have two houses, so Canadian troops occupied our little Lancing house. I don't know if the government purchased it from my father, but we never got it back.

Just before the war, we had all been issued these gas masks in these little square boxes. I don't know what sort of gas this was going to shield us from, but I guess it gave them a sort of confidence in a way. So we repaired back to London again. My father had become an air raid warden and my sister, although she was still working on Fleet Street, had become a volunteer Red Cross nurse. I don't know why Sylvia became a Red Cross nurse because she couldn't stand the sight of blood. We were all told in case of a bomb dropping near you, it's quite feasible that it may knock out the water mains, then you would have no water; so be sure to fill all bathtubs, your basins, your sinks, your pots and pans with water so you have a supply. If you made a cup of tea, refill the kettle again. This is what we did at this shop that the WVS had taken over.

The so-called kitchen was on the upper floor. It was very cold because there was no heating of any kind. So the day I was going to make tea, I went up and plugged in the electric kettle. Within seconds steam was coming out of it. I thought, *Good heavens, the person before me didn't refill the kettle.* So I unplugged it, took it over to the sink and took the lid off to fill it with water. Of course, all the steam came gushing out and burnt both my hands. I dropped the kettle and broke it. I couldn't do anything from the shock of it. I remember looking out of a window, thrusting my hands in my pockets because they were shaking so much, then a few minutes later thought, *Well, I've got to go and tell them,* so I went downstairs. I said, "I'm terribly sorry. I'm afraid I dropped the kettle." They were very annoyed with me because all the factories were turned over to building aircraft, bombs and things. You just couldn't pop into the hardware store and buy another kettle.

They were way underground, very doubly annoyed with me. Tears started coming out of my eyes as I took my hands out of my coat to dry my tears, the skin came off both of the back of my hands. Everybody was shocked and said, "Good heavens." The skin had just burned off my hand. My sister flapped the skin back over and bandaged my hands up. I don't know why it didn't occur to the family to take me to the hospital or the doctors or anything. That evening they took me to the cinema to keep my mind off my burns. The actresses in the movie were just squabbling and bickering the whole time. It was the last thing I wanted to soothe my nerves. I never forgot that film. Because my parents were trying to be sweet and had taken me there, I pretended to like it, but the whole time I was in agony with my hands. That was the first of my war wounds.

Our art school got quite a number of refugee students. At our coffee breaks, we would all sit around and they would tell us about the terrible things that were happening in their countries—Poland, Czech-oslovakia—all the other countries that had been taken over by Hitler. We were just horrified to listen to such; to know that people could be so beastly to other people—just ruin lives and homes. The destruction was terrible. I felt so sorry for them because here they were in a foreign country, having to learn a new language, not used to our customs, with no homes, and had no idea what had happened to their relatives. It was a terrible time. We felt so badly about their situation. The young men who were old enough at art school were all signing up to go in one of the services. One of them who had the means of being quite a very good artist, volunteered for the RAF as a pilot. He came back from the recruiting office very dejected. We asked, "What happened?" He said, "They turned me down because I'm color blind," and, of course, we were amazed and said, "How can you be a painter and nobody know that you're color blind?"

But I did notice that one of our art masters, Robert Buhler, who actually was of German-Swiss extraction but been brought up in England, when he painted, he used a lot of white paint, so everything had a dull look about it. I thought, *I wonder if he's color blind, too.* He made a very successful career as an artist, so like Thomas Kinkade (who I think has those dreary paintings). People think they are so wonderful, but he uses a lot of white paint in there; made them look gloomy, to me anyway.[1]

Then we went down to the coast again. A family we got to know who had these amateur play companies had a son named Peter who had joined the RAF and had been sent to Australia to train, which seems an awfully long way to go. I know some RAF trainees who went to America and Canada. When he came back after finishing his training, he said, "They're so short of actors there that while I was there I did quite a few stints on the radio. They said if I ever wanted a job at the end of the war to come back, I'd have one waiting for me." So that was his future—secured, hopefully.

An MP named Sir John Anderson had passed a bill that we were all to be issued an Anderson Shelter, which is a sort of tin arrangement that one had to sort of partially put in the ground, digging under it. You would get in and supposedly be sheltered from a bomb dropping on you.[2] And so there went our croquet lawn. That became our air raid shelter. My father planted vegetables on one part of the front of his garden, which was quite large. He went to Woolworth and bought a package of cabbage seeds. He planted this

---

[1] Robert Buhler RA (1916–1989) was born in London to Swiss parents. He was a member of the Royal Academy from 1946. Source: http://www.belgraviagallery.com/artist/robert-buhler/, accessed April 16, 2013

[2] The Anderson shelter was designed in 1938 by William Paterson and Oscar Carl (Karl) Kerrison in response to a request from the Home Office. It was named after Sir John Anderson, then Lord Privy Seal with special responsibility for preparing air-raid precautions immediately prior to the outbreak of World War II, and it was he who then initiated the development of the shelter ... Anderson shelters were designed to accommodate up to six people. The main principle of protection was based on curved and straight galvanised corrugated steel panels. Six curved panels were bolted together at the top, so forming the main body of the shelter, three straight sheets on either side, and two more straight panels were fixed to each end, one containing the door—a total of fourteen panels. A small drainage sump was often incorporated in the floor to collect rainwater seeping into the shelter. The shelters were 6 ft (1.8 m) high, 4 ft 6 in (1.4 m) wide, and 6 ft 6 in (2 m) long. They were buried 4 ft (1.2 m) deep in the soil and then covered with a minimum of 15 in (0.4 m) of soil above the roof. The earth banks could be planted with vegetables and flowers, that at times could be quite an appealing sight and in this way would become the subject of competitions of the best-planted shelter among householders in the neighborhood. Source: http://en.wikipedia.org/wiki/Air-raid_shelter, April 16, 2013

whole area and in no time at all had these huge cabbages. I don't know what type they were, but they were absolutely gigantic—three feet across. I remember once seeing a policeman walking down the road. He must of had one of father's cabbages because you couldn't see him. You could only see his feet walking along as the cabbage was so huge. The cabbages overtook the whole garden and could feed an army. Father was inclined to lean over his garden gate and beg anybody, "Hey, would you like a cabbage?" That was part of his war effort, supplying the local people with cabbage.

Anderson Shelter

Of course, this was the beginning of what was referred to as the "Phoney War" because all sorts of rumors went around that we were going to be attacked immediately; so we were used to sirens going off. When they first went off, one's heart would sink to one's stomach, then you realized that no, a flock of birds had gone by and they just had set off the alarm. In the end, we decided it was just too much night-after-night going down, huddling inside this tin capsule thing, probably dying of pneumonia, so we decided we would rather die in a warm bed and gave up the shelter. Our cat used to sleep in there. Other than that, it remained empty.

Chapter Seven

HOUSE BOMBED, NURSE TERRY, KINGSTON-UPON-THAMES, GRAND PIANO

I think most people decided that was not the way to go. Then one night, the usual siren went off. We were all in bed, when suddenly I was awoken by a huge bang. It sounded like a sheet being ripped apart. Then the whole house seemed to be lifted up and slammed down again. The plaster from the ceiling came all over my bed. I tottered out of the bed to go to the bathroom to try and wash this off, and I couldn't open the door because the ceiling had fallen in. Fortunately in England, we do not, or we did not in those days, have the WC (water closet), toilet, or whatever you want to call it, inside the bathroom. It was separate, thank goodness for that, because the ceiling hadn't fallen in on that little room. We used it quite a lot.

My father walked through the house and saw ceilings down; some parts of the house obliterated. He said, "Well, obviously we can't stay here. We will have to leave. Collect your clothes and come." We said, "What about our things?" He said, "I will see if

I can get them down." So much had been smashed, so much of my school certificates that I fought so hard to get fell off the wall, crashed and smashed. I had a lot of things; also a diary I had been keeping. That went up in smoke, so we had to leave, never to return to that area again where I grew up, went to church, was confirmed and had all my friends. We just had to walk away. My father moved us to a country town.

Guilford (Surrey) was quite a large market town. Father found a rather gaunt looking Victorian or Edwardian house on the residential side of the town, which was on a hill. The house had several floors and had a deaconess at the local Anglican church living on the top floor, so the rest of the floors were for our benefit. We rented this place, having what my father could retrieve of our furniture sent down to us. About the most useless of the things that arrived was this concert grand piano. It was a Bechstein or a Steinway. Nobody had time to play it then anyway. Amazingly enough there was not a chip or scratch on it. How it escaped damage, I don't know. We had big enough rooms to accommodate it in this house, which had a very long garden which went right down to the next street a block away.

Sylvia by then had gone to a hospital in Cornwall, which was called the Headland Hospital. It was right on the Cornish coast, like a peninsula sticking out in the sea, where officers who lost their limbs went to recuperate. That's what Sylvia was doing at that time. My mother had decided that she was going to work for the London County Council in the Docklands area of London, evacuating people who were bombed out of their homes; providing accommodation for them until they could be sent on a train to the country.

I decided I better do something, too. Obviously, there was no art school there, so I couldn't continue with my art studies. I had been at the art school for three years and was about to set for my exams to go to the Royal College of Art where I would eventually get my degree, but Hitler put pay to that.

When I was seventeen, I was supposed to go to Switzerland for finishing school. I didn't regret not being able to do that. But I did regret, if you are keen on flying when you're seventeen, not having flying lessons. Of course, I couldn't do that either, but I had to do something. I made a friend in Guilford. She said she was going to work as a nurse's aide in the big hospital at Royal Surrey County Hospital. I thought, *Well, I will do that, too*, not having any idea what it involved. So we both toddled along there and they told us the hours would be very long. We got one day off every ninth day, but if the sirens sounded, we had to go back on duty again. Mother was most indignant about this and thought 16 year-old girls needed a complete day off every nine days. She wrote her member of Parliament and apprised him of the situation. He got in touch with the hospital authorities who graciously allowed us to have a full day off. I was very popular with the other nurses' aides but not with the hospital administration.

Terry in WWII nurse's uniform.

When I first went there, we had accommodation near the hospital; on the top floor. Someone put a sign on the door saying

"The Nursery" because we were all sixteen (I just turned 17 at the time). We used to go to work with the outpatients. All I remember doing is taking first aid classes, home nursing and crawling around a Quonset hut. We had to crawl across the floor to learn how to survive in a smoke-filled room.

Everybody had been asked if they had a spare room in their house and to register it with the town hall as there was a Canadian regiment about 15 miles away. For R&R they could go to the twinkling lights of the market town of Guilford. There was a YMCA there for the men, but no accommodation for the officers. So we registered ours, since we had several rooms vacant.

One night my father and I stood on the hill looking at the horizon, which was London in the distance, and the sky was ablaze. It was just on fire, mainly in the Docklands section because that's where the Germans were aiming particularly, at the docks, so that we would not get provisions brought in to us from other countries. We knew that Mother was in the middle of all that, which made us very apprehensive. When we went to pick up Mother from the station every morning, we didn't know until she got off the train that she had survived that day. She would have a few hours rest and back she would go again to that inferno. She came back one day in great distress. She said, "I really can't hear at all now." We asked, "What happened?" And she said, "Well, last night I was standing at the top of the stairs." (It was a multi-story, public school that had been evacuated and everything was concrete.) "I had just seen a family into a room upstairs, standing at the top of the concrete stairs, and a bomb fell in the next road. The vibration, the concussion, threw me down the stairs and I hit my head on the wall." So poor Mother lost most of her hearing at that time and had to get a hearing aid.

The day before, my mother had brought my grandmother, rather irascible old Irish lady, down from London to get away from the bombing. My parents had decided the best place for her to be was in the ground floor in the kitchen area, which had been originally for the cook/housekeeper. It had a bedroom and a bathroom to save her from going up the stairs. The next night, my father and I were having something to eat when suddenly the sirens went off. I said, "Oh, dear, I'm going to have to go back to the hospital," although it was my day off. As I slammed on my helmet, it started to rain. I ran down the hill not realizing it was "blackout," so I couldn't see anything. I didn't see I had gotten to the bottom yet. There was a huge double sided Victorian mailbox at the bottom and I hit my nose on the rim of it. Of course, I staggered back, my face immediately became swollen, and blood was pouring down. The sensible thing to do was to go back home again, but *no*, I was Joan of Arc or something. *I must go on*, I thought, so I staggered on until I got to the junction. I was about to cross the bridge over to the county hospital, when I tripped over something in the dark and my helmet fell off. Well, there was an "Ack-Ack" (air defense) gun outside the hospital (next to a sign that read, "Quiet Please") firing away and I didn't want to be hit by shrapnel. I was groping around for my helmet, but because my face was so swollen I could hardly see. The air warden came out and said, "What are you doing out here?" berating me. I said, "I'm looking for my helmet." And so the officer found it and slapped it on my head. But as it was full of water by then, I looked particularly bedraggled apart from my bloody nose. They said, "What are you doing out here?" I said, "Well, I'm going on duty at the hospital." They laughed. They said, "You look more like a victim than a nurse." So much sympathy from them!

I got even less sympathy when I got into the Outpatients where we were going to receive people wounded from the bombing. They rushed up to me, "What happened? What happened? Where was the incident?" I said, "Oh, incident? Oh, no, I hit my head on the rim of a mailbox." They lost interest immediately. "Oh, well, you better go and wipe it up, then roll some bandages, I suppose." We had other things to think about. That was my second war wound. I sat there trying to see everything through squinty little eyes, rolled bandages and made tea for people. Then the "all clear" sounded, so I thought I'd go home. At least Father will have a cup of tea for me and I will feel better.

I went home but I was having to avoid lots of rubble everywhere, dust from the rubble of the trees and houses being demolished. I had to pick my way back across to the residential area. I climbed up the hill until I came to the bottom of our road, but it was cordoned off with barriers. There were police and army there. I said, "What's happened?" They told me, "There's been an incident." My heart sank as I asked, "What sort of an incident?" He said, "Well there's an unexploded bomb in one of those houses." So I said, "Oh, which house?" And he said, "Well, where do you live?" And I said, "Highlands." He said, "Oh, that's where the incident is." Then I said, "Well, what happened to my father?" He said, "Well, everybody has been evacuated. They have gone down to the town hall."

So I tottered down to the town hall. I thought, *This is too much*! and fought my way through a throng of people to find my father who rushed up to me and said, "Oh, my darling, what's happened?" He thought I was part of the bombing incident. So I assured him, no, I did it my own silly way. He brought me a cup of tea and he said, "Well, there is a lighter side to this." I said, "There is a lighter side to this?" He pointed to my grandmother, who was sitting, all four-foot-eleven of her, sitting bolt upright in a chair very grimly staring ahead. Beside her stood a very large Canadian officer. He had come, after I had gone and after my grandmother had gone to bed, to stay the night in one of our rooms. My father said, "When this bomb fell, our ARP warden knocked on the door and said, 'You will have to evacuate at once.'" So they both rushed the door. Then my father belatedly remembered my grandmother and said, "Oh, my mother-in-law is in the downstairs bedroom," and he turned to get her, but the Canadian said, "I will get her. You go get the car." My father went out and got the car. He had the door open and out comes this large Canadian holding my grandmother in his arms and her little feet are waving in the air and her fists are beating this poor man on the chest and saying, "Who are you, young man? How dare you? Let me down. Let me down at once." The poor thing was very deaf. I could just imagine her being scooped up out of her sleep by this large person and nobody being an able to communicate with her. So they put her in the car seat next to my father who sort of patted her on the shoulder. She said, "I'm not amused. I'm not a bit amused."

Fortunately, when we went to meet Mother off the train the next morning, the junction was still standing. We had to tell her, "Sorry, Mummy, we have to go live somewhere else. We have been bombed again." We lost more China and more artifacts again, but one thing that was not a bit damaged was that darn piano. Seems strange that my father would decide to move back to the London area, but he said, "Well, anywhere we go it seems we could be exposed." He had found an apartment overlooking the Thames at Surbiton, which was centrally heated. Coal was severely rationed when it came to heating our houses. My father said an apartment is going to be easy to heat, as these apartments had central heating. That was our third move. We were overlooking the Thames and Hampton Court Palace grounds in a corner flat, which was quite pleasant viewing.

On the opposite side of the road, in Kingston-Upon-Thames, was a similar block of flats. The road divided Surbiton and Kingston-Upon-Thames. Next door to those block of flats were some Victorian mansions. Orphans from the Low Country, I believe it was Belgium, were in one of those houses. The orphanage was run by nuns. A bomb landed on that house and destroyed it, and the explosion shook the block of flats my parents lived in. The impact sort of lifted the flat and dumped it back down again, so nothing—doors, windows—nothing fit well after that. A lot of the windows were blown out. Since glass panes were hard to come by, they had to board up the windows with wood panels, which didn't keep out the cold wind coming straight off the Thames, and my mother was suffering from pleurisy.

That darn grand piano was in my parents' bedroom. It just fit in the bay window. My father said, "Well, we obviously can't stay here." So we moved across the hall to an inside flat; our fourth move. There was no way that we could put the grand piano in the new flat, so my father had to give it to a local service canteen because nobody wanted to buy a concert grand piano during the war. I guess there were beer mugs put on the grand piano while they sang around it. That was finally the end of the grand piano. Sadly, that bomb destroyed the Victorian house that housed the orphans who had escaped from Belgium. They were all killed. What a tragedy.

In the middle of the river opposite our apartment was a little island called Ravens Ait. Ait stands for "River Island". I suppose originally there were ravens on it, but since well before the war there was a large two-story building there which had been what they called a roadhouse where people could ferry over and have dancing. The *SS Neptune* was a training ship on land for sea scouts, who reported from the east end of London. It gave them a breath of fresh air, and it was quite amusing to hear them blowing their whistles, watch them learn to tie knots, sail along in little boats and learn seamanship with bugles going, et cetera. Not very peaceful in peacetime, I suppose, but we quite enjoyed watching them. There was a little ferry, one man and a boat, that could take you across from our side, the Surrey side of the Thames, over to the

Middlesex side of the Thames through a back gate entrance to the gardens of Hampton Court Palace.

Deer and sheep grazed there, which made it bucolic when you think that we were only about twenty miles from Piccadilly Circus. A lot of people took their dogs for walks on the grounds there. They had to have the dogs on leashes to keep them well away from where the sheep and the deer were. Sometimes we would just walk out to the back of Hampton Court Palace. The side that we saw, coming from the other side of the Thames, was the William & Mary side, which was a sort of stucco. If you went on the front entrance going into Hampton Court Palace, that was the Tudor side. It was quite a remarkable building, of course, with the usual ghost of Anne Boleyn and several others. I think I understand that Cardinal Woolsey built it for himself as a summer home from London and got in bad odor with King Henry the Eighth. So he pretended he built it for Henry and presented it to him. Henry the Eighth used that as his summer home, twenty miles from London.[1]

---

[1] The Knights Hospitallers of St John Jerusalem acquired the manor of Hampton in 1236 and used the site as a grange—a center for their agricultural estates.... The first tenant we know much about was the courtier Giles Daubeney, who took out a lease on the property in 1494.... Daubeney was on the way up (he became Lord Chamberlain to King Henry VII the following year), and needed a house close to London.... Little is known about Daubeney's Hampton Court, but the value of the property increased considerably during his short tenure (he died in 1508). But any improvements Daubeney made were quickly eclipsed by the ambitions of Hampton Court's next occupant, Thomas Wolsey.... By the late 1520s, Henry was desperate to obtain a divorce from his first wife. Katherine had failed (in Henry's eyes) to provide Henry with a male heir, despite numerous pregnancies. Katherine was 40 in 1525, and the object of Henry's desire was now the much younger Anne Boleyn. But after years of political maneuvering and discussions, Katherine still refused to comply, the Pope didn't grant the divorce and in 1528 Wolsey lost both Hampton Court and York Place to the King. Source: Historic Royal Palaces: Hampton Court Palace, http://www.hrp.org.uk/HamptonCourtPalace, accessed April 18, 2013

Chapter Eight

RKO STUDIOS, DOG FIGHT, THE WAFF

We got to know our immediate neighbors quite well. The couple who lived above us were Ernest and Maude (Maudy) Simon and their daughter Pat, who was away at boarding school. Ernest was a rather tall rangy rather stooped-over man, Jewish, and we called him Springhill Jack because, as he walked along, he bounced. We felt he must have had springs on his heels. He sort of would lope along. His wife, Maude, was quite diminutive. She said she was descended from Bonny Prince Charlie. As I understand, Prince Charles never married. We went up there for coffee one day. They had a grand piano and lots of photos on top of it, but they were all of Ernest when he was with RKO Studios in England. There was a photo of him with Walt Disney, with other producers and directors and film stars, and none really of anybody else in the family. They also a Church of England hymnbook. I wondered why they had a hymnbook on top of their piano and concluded that it was unfortunate that in England there was still a sort of prejudice especially against middle class Jews, which was left over,

I suppose, from the time hundreds of years ago when the Jews were banned from Britain all together.[1]

Ernest was doing everything he could to point out that he was actually a Christian, and we liked him anyway. It didn't matter what he was, but I asked my father, "Do you think they had singsongs around the piano using the hymnbook?" He said no, it was just to point out to us that he was an Anglican and didn't go to the synagogue. I thought it was rather sad that these Jewish people had to try and be non-Jewish to get along with the white British people. Anyway, we liked them very much. Maudy and my mother, between them, opened up one of the empty shops in Surbiton and raised money for the air sea rescue fund. They had great success. It was amazing the number of people that brought in silver, serving china and other expensive things to donate. It was run like a thrift shop where you could go in and buy these things. You didn't want to accumulate too much china and have it smashed as we did with all our bombings, so people didn't go out of their way to acquire more at that time.

One day Mother went up to London to the RKO Studio offices to ask if they would contribute to the funds for air and sea rescue. She was shown into this ornate office with a huge desk which Ernest was sitting behind. When she came in, he was busy on the phone to this and the other person. About five minutes later, having been supplied with a cup of coffee by his secretary, he finally got around to saying, "Yes, and what can I do for you?" very condescendingly. He was all business like. Anyway, they did contribute, which was great.

---

1 In 1290, King Edward I issued an edict expelling all Jews from England. The expulsion edict remained in force for the rest of the Middle Ages. The edict was not an isolated incident, but the culmination of over 200 years of conflict on the matters of usury. Oliver Cromwell encouraged Jews to return to England in 1657, over 350 years since their banishment by Edward I, in the hope that they would help speed up the recovery of the country after the disruption of the Civil Wars. Source: http://en.wikipedia.org/wiki/Edict_of_Expulsion, accessed April 18, 2013

As a nurses' aide I mostly fetched bedpans and gave drinks to patients, anything the nurses wanted me to do, but it was a very distressing environment to work in. Some of the soldiers in hospital were at Dunkirk. When they were being evacuated they were picked up by an oil tanker that had been dive bombed by the Germans. The men who fell into the burning oil that spread out on the water around the ship had terrible burn injuries. One young man, about 19, was put on a bed with a circular ring around it, and every hour he had to be turned so that he wouldn't develop bedsores. Every time he was turned, he screamed, even though he was on morphine.

In their wisdom, the hospital authorities had put in a separate ward on the same floor for a German bomber crew that had been shot down. They had to put guards on the doors because the British infantry soldiers wanted to get at them.

One day I was on duty, during the Battle of Britain, we heard a dog fight going on overhead. I ran out into the courtyard. Right overhead was a Messerschmitt and a Spitfire. It was very exciting. The sky was an absolute brilliant blue with not a cloud in sight, but it looked like a giant child had scrawled all over the sky where the vapor trails from the planes were suspended. We were fascinated by this until the machine gun clips of spent bullets started dropping down on us, and we rushed in side.

About that time they lowered the age limit for joining the service from 18 to 17. At this time, Sylvia was with a BBC overseas service being evacuated to Evesham in Worcestershire. They lived in a big house that had been taken over by the BBC with all these different nationalities from Romania to Russia living there and broadcasting to the various countries. Sylvia spoke several languages so I don't know which country she was broadcasting to. That's where she met her first husband.

She told me, "You know, it's not going to be long before they will be conscripting every able-bodied person and you will have no choice where to go. You might be sent to a factory, or you might have to go and work on the land." I said, "Well, in that case I think I will join the service." Of course, without a doubt, I was going to join the Women's Auxiliary Air Force, which was attached to the Royal Air Force. So I trotted up to the headquarters, and an officer said, "Well, now, what can you do?" I wasn't going to tell her I was studying art because I could see myself having to do camouflage painting for the rest of the war. So I said, "I'm in school still." She said, "Can you cook?" I said, "No." "Can you drive?" I said, "No. I'm not old enough to have a license." After she went through quite a few things, she said, "Then I suppose we better put you into special duties." I said, "What is that?" She said, "You will be a plotter." And I said, "What does that mean?" She said, "I really can't tell you because it's a secret and it's on a need-to-know basis. I don't know. You will be designated as potential officer material." I thought afterwards, *Isn't that typical? I can't do anything, but they are going to put me in the realm of being an officer.*

> Communications should be addresse... in Charge,
> and the following Reference ... ted :—
> WF/...
>
> From :—London & S.E. Area Recruiting H.Q.　　　Telephone :
> Women's Auxiliary Air Force,　　　　　　　　HOLBORN 3434.
> Victory House, Kingsway, W.C.2.　　　　　　　Ex. ...
>
> To :—Miss ..Terry-Smith,　　　12th May　1941.
> Highlands,
> Sydney Rd.,
> Guildford, Surrey.
>
> Madam,
>
> With reference to your application for enrolment into the Women's Auxiliary Air Force, will you please forward to this Headquarters Certificate of Release from the First Aid Post, Surrey County Hospital, together with the attached Form 76, duly completed.
>
> I am, Madam,
>
> *[signature]*
> O. I/c W.A.A.F.,
> For Officer Commanding
> London & S.E. Area Recruiting H.Q.

Letter from WAFF recruiting headquarters, 1941.

STEPHEN DOSTER

A.M. Pamphlet 103
3rd Edition

WOMEN'S AUXILIARY AIR FORCE
Notes for the Information of Candidates

1. Age Limits.
 (i) A candidate must have attained the age of 18 but must not have reached the age of 44. Those who served in the Women's Auxiliary Army Corps, Women's Royal Air Force, or similar service in the last war may be accepted up to the age of 50.
 (ii) Candidates for enrolment for clerks special duties and radio operator must not have reached the age of 36.

2. Medical Examination.
 A candidate will be required to undergo a medical examination by a R.A.F. medical officer or civil medical practitioner appointed by the Air Ministry for this purpose, and must attain the medical standard of fitness laid down.

3. Period of Engagement.
 A candidate will be enrolled for the duration of the war.

4. Enrolment.
 Candidates will normally be enrolled only if their civilian qualifications fit them for the particular trade in which they wish to be enrolled. The trades for which candidates may be accepted are as follows (the trades are placed in the groups indicated for purposes of pay (see para. 8)):—

Group II.	Group III.	Group IV.	Group V.	Group M.
Instrument mechanic, W T (Slip Reader) operator, Sparking plug tester, Wireless operator.	Cook, Fabric worker, Aero, Fabric worker, Ballers.	Equipment assistant, Clerk Special duties ,, General duties ,, Pay accounting ,, Equipment accounting, Administrative, Telegraphist operator, Radio operator, Charging board operator, R T operator, Fitter.	Telephone operator, M.T. driver, Aircraftsman. ,, General duties, ,, Works ops. ,, Waitress, ,, Orderly.	Dental Clerk Orderly, Sick quarters attendant.

*Group II after 6 months efficient service.

5. Rank on Entry and Promotion.
 Recruits will be entered in the rank of aircraftwoman 2nd class, and will be eligible for promotion when qualified, as vacancies arise. Recruits who require technical training will be enrolled as aircraftshands under training, and will be placed in Group V (see para. 8). Officers will normally be selected from the ranks.

6. Obligations.
 A recruit will accept the following obligations:—
 (i) To serve in any part of the United Kingdom and overseas.
 (ii) To obey all orders given by her superior officers, or those who may be placed in authority over her.
 (iii) To perform any work which may be required of her by her superior officers.

7. Discipline.
 (i) While serving with the Royal Air Force when on active service, an airwoman is subject to the Air Force Act and may, by reason of her employment, become subject to such penalties as may be prescribed by law for offences committed in breach of her contract of service.
 (ii) A recruit guilty of any act of neglect in breach of her contract of service or of any of the rules, regulations or instructions laid down from time to time, will be liable to any of the following minor punishments, to be awarded by such authority (male or female) that the Air Council shall appoint:—
  (a) Extra duties.
  (b) Restriction of privileges.
  (c) Admonition.
 (iii) The services of an airwoman may be terminated:—
  (a) forthwith on account of misconduct or breach of conditions;
  (b) on 15 days' notice being given:—
   (i) on account of medical unfitness;
   (ii) if it appears unlikely that she will become efficient in her duties;
   (iii) if her services are no longer required.

8. Financial Provisions.
 (i) Pay.—Airwomen will receive pay for each day on which they perform duty or are absent on authorised leave at the rates set out below; except that all airwomen who

WAFF candidate information.

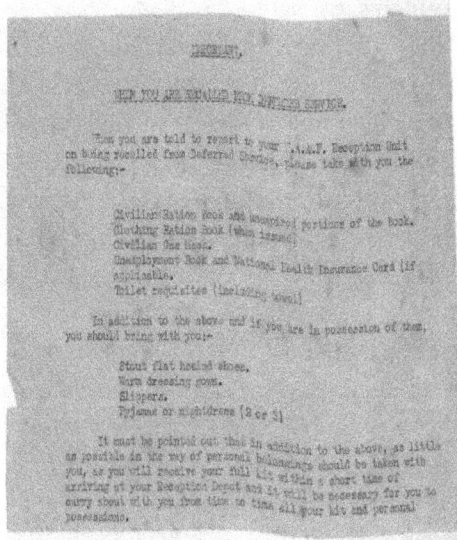

WAFF report to duty notice.

WWII RAF Operations Room

I asked her where I would be stationed, and she said, "There in the Operations Room for the airfield." I thought, *Great. I'll be near all these planes and will be able to see them up close.* What I didn't realize is that during the Battle of Britain so many Ops Rooms

[Operations Rooms] at the RAF bases had been damaged that they moved the Ops Rooms miles away from the actual airfields.

She said, "But you must not tell anybody what you're doing." I said, "I must tell them something." She said, "Yes, you're a clerk, special duties, doing clerical work." So I went home and told my parents, "I'm going to do clerical work." My father said, "What does that involve?" I said, "I don't know. Filing things, I suppose." He said, "Well, what is the special duties in that?" And I said, "Well, I think they must be classified files." I had no idea. I was really floundering.

Off I went to this camp near Cheltenham, which at that time was a growing yet sedate Georgian town with retired officers and their ladies. For two weeks we trained, we marched, rather pathetically. I mean, I had to learn how to march, different forms we had to fill in if we wanted this, that and the other, how to salute and obey your officer and all sorts of restricting things that I didn't anticipate.

A few days before the two weeks were up, my mother came down to see what was happening to her little darling. She asked permission if I could go and have tea and dinner with her. So I was given permission, and as it was the weekend, I could take someone with me, so I took another girl. We went to tea at the Estate Dainty Tea Rooms with a proper copper kettle and warming pans on the walls; the waitresses were all middle-aged ladies wearing smocks. For ten days beforehand I had been issued these heavy china mugs that when full of tea or coffee or whatever, it was so heavy to pick up I had to use both hands. So when we were having tea at this dainty tearoom, I picked up my teacup, forgetting that it wasn't a heavy mug, and the tea shot right over my shoulder, fortunately missing the person sitting at the next table. My mother was shocked and said, "Oh, you have only been in the WAAF ten days and look what's happened to you." She was mortified.

That night she took me to dinner at the only hotel in the town that the other ranks were forbidden to go to. This was something new to me. After the war, when I had come to America, I thought, "I'm sure this must be how black Americans felt when they were denied going into certain restaurants or shops or swimming pools. I suddenly realized that if you're of a certain rank you can't go into restaurants or places that you could before until you go on leave and you're in civilian clothes, then, of course, you can. It was just crazy.

Anyway Mother took me to this hotel where most of the dining room used to be filled with WAAF or RAF officers, and here I was this lowly WAAF. I sank down in my chair, and said, "Mummy, why did you choose this one hotel?" She said, "It's the only decent hotel in town. Where else would I go?" Oh, well, got to love her.

I shared a Nissen [Quonset] hut with about 12 other girls, a rather motley crew. One of them had been a teacher and another had been a gym mistress. She used to wake up every morning saying, "Here we are again, bleary-eyed and blotto [drunk]." We didn't appreciate her humor. There was an admiral's daughter, and then there was this girl that told me she was an actress. I stood in awe of her giving up her career for the war. I said to one of the others, "That girl over there is an actress," and she said, "Well, let's be generous and say she calls herself an actress," meaning, a call-girl. And I said, "Well, what else would she be?" Oh, dear, how innocent I was.

About four days before we graduated, so to speak, we who were going to be in special duties had to sit before a panel of people who asked questions like, "Do you get claustrophobic?" and things like that, which made us all very nervous because we had no idea what we were going to do, why they were asking if we were claustrophobic and these other peculiar questions. One by one we had to go into a room with a psychiatrist who showed us ink blots and things, and we had to identify them. He asked, "How would you be in a crisis? Would you be able to cope?" I thought, "How would I know?" Except for the time when I nearly floated out to sea, I never remember being in a crisis. I suppose the bombings were crises, but anyway I didn't know quite what he meant.

We all passed and had four days leave. I went home to my parents and shocked them when I said, "I'm being sent to Lancashire where they talk funny and eat peculiar food." It might have been Siberia as far as I was concerned. I think it was all of 90 miles away. But in those days the speed limit was 30 miles-an-hour, and nearly all the roads were just converted cart tracks that wound in and out of fields and hedges. You couldn't drive fast anyway, so nobody really, unless they were going on a holiday or something, went very far. I don't think I had ever been further north than Oxfordshire or Cambridgeshire, so I certainly never had been up that far north in the midlands, which is laughable when you think how small Britain is anyway. In those days we stayed close to home, so I was horrified that I was going out to Lancashire, and I thought, *What good am I going to do in the service up in Lancashire?* I was soon to find out.

Chapter Nine

SPEKE (1941), "DUMMY RUN," THE BIG SECRET

Six of us got on a train in London to Liverpool. We were met by a female sergeant who said, "Now, you are going to be stationed at the Speke Aerodrome in operations. Although your station is Speke, which is in Liverpool, you will be stationed out in the country, in Aughton Springs, where you will be billeted, and your Operations Room will be about five miles beyond there. But I need one of you to go to 9 Group Headquarters in Preston for two weeks to replace somebody until they get a relief." I was standing next to this sergeant, and she said, "You'll do." It was like being thrown out of the nest.

I thought I could cope with whatever was going to happen as long as I'm with the others, but I was separated from them; taken to this place in Lancashire where I was going to be billeted. From there I had to get on a bus, which took me to a long driveway that led to the entrance of a huge Victorian mansion. There was a guard outside, and he said, "What are you doing here?" I said, "I have an appointment with the flight lieutenant." I forget what his name was. The guard opened the door for me and called some clerical chap who was walking down, "This young lady has come to see Lieutenant," I say his name is Wellington, "Flight Lieutenant Wellington," and the chap said, "Oh, you poor kid." I laughed and asked, "Why?" He said, "Oh, you will find out." He took me up this very grand staircase. When we got to the top, we walked a little way along the corridor of the first floor, and when we got to the door he said, "I will just tell you that he's a misogynist. He doesn't like women, and he doesn't like women in the service." He added, "He's also an earl." I thought, *What does that signify? Does he have a dungeon in the basement that recalcitrant WAAFs are thrown in or something?*

I was quaking in my shoes by the time I got in the door, which was a very small room with a glass panel in front of it. To me, at that time it was like looking out on something on that movie that came out right before the war, H. G. Wells' ***Things To Come***. The whole inside of the building had been scooped out; there were just glass booths at the different levels where the floors should be. Down on the very ground floor was a huge table with a map of that whole area where there were these WAAF and RAF men sitting around it. Nothing was happening at that time, so they were reading books or whatever. Here was Flight Lieutenant Wellington glaring at me. He said, "I suppose it's too much to hope you're Welsh." I said, "No, I'm sorry, I'm from London." "Oh, London," he said, as if that was a den of iniquity. I said, "Does it matter that I'm not Welsh?" He said, "Well, my group headquarters covers most of the midlands and part of Wales. You will have to learn the Welsh town names," (which as everybody knows have very few vowels). So I had to learn Pwllehli and Machynlleth and all of these guttural sounding places.

He said, "Now our function is air raid warnings." He sat in front of the console panel with all these knobs. Around the knobs were different colors, and over the top the knobs were the names of these towns and cities. He said, "Now what you have to do is if we get a warning of a raid coming, you have to turn each knob one at a time to the right; that's air raid warning yellow. Wait a minute, I think it was air raid warning red, and then you say, 'Machynlleth, air raid warning, air raid warning red,' and then you go on to the next town, to Liverpool, Manchester and so forth and so on. Then when you get to the last one, you go back to the top again and say, 'Machynlleth, air raid warning purple,' then you go through all the others. When he got to the bottom one, I said, "But by the time you get to the bottom one, isn't the air raid already over then?" I had forgotten all about not questioning your officer and obeying them blindly. He said, "Have you got a better idea?" I said, "Of course not. I only just sat down here. But surely, you know, that's a problem." He said, "I will deal with the problem. Now, we will practice this and we will do a dummy run of it."

So I started to put my hand on a knob, and I said, "But should I not preface this with 'This is dummy run?'" He raised his hand and said, "Have you not been told not to argue with your officers?" I said, "I'm not arguing, sir. I'm asking a question." He said, "Do exactly what I say. I'm telling you to call Machynlleth and tell them air raid warning red, okay?" I said, "Yes, sir." So I went through all this. Well, halfway through me turning the knobs and saying "Air raid warning red," there was a lot of activity in all the other booths, you know, with the representatives of the Navy, the Army and different services. They were all starting to ring him up, and he got sort of red in the face saying, "Well, I'm sorry I've got a new girl and she's just learning." I was so indignant. Then he put the phone down and said, "Quick, get back in there and say, 'Air raid all clear.'" So I did that rapidly, and he said, "Are you aware, ACW Terry-Smith, that you have just stopped the war effort in its tracks?" I said, "What do you mean?" He said, "All these factories had to close down and send their people down into the basements to the air raid shelters." I said, "But I asked you, sir, and you said"—and he held up his hand and said magnanimously, "Well, say no more," because he knew clearly he was in the wrong.

For the next two weeks we sort of had a silent truce. When the replacement came (I had replaced a younger man, who was sent overseas), they had gotten an older RAF personnel chap. He was probably rather amazed that both of us practically fell on him with relief. The flight lieutenant was getting rid of this pesky girl, and I was going to go back to Speke.

So I was given transportation and taken up to Aughton Springs. We were billeted in a millionaire's house, which had been taken over by the RAF. It had beautiful grounds with two full-time gardeners. We had our own kitchen staff and ate in their grand dining room. Our bathrooms had floor-to-ceiling mirrors and gold taps. We even had batwomen [personal servants usually assigned to commissioned officers] who made our beds and cleaned our bedrooms—and *we* were the lowest of the low. In fact, most of the people waiting on us were corporals or sergeants. So we felt rather sort of embarrassed about that situation. However, sometime later, conscription came in and we lost our batwomen, so we had to make our own beds, poor dears. But this left ill feelings for the rest of the war between us, the plotters and special duties, and the rest of the WAFF rank, because they thought we were snobs; a position we didn't really put ourselves in.

In the smaller fighter station Ops Rooms we had three watches, about ten of us on each watch, so there would be close to thirty Ops girls at Speke. The largest stations had four watches, about fifty or sixty of us. That's why we were always billeted in houses with just us in it because we were there 24 hours between the watches. There was always either somebody coming off duty, getting ready to go on duty or going on 24 hour leave. So with all that turmoil they couldn't put us with the other WAAF. That also sort of made for rather awkward situations with them.

I think I had been in the WAFF about six weeks when I was offered an admin [Administration] commission. It didn't seem to matter that one made big booboos like I did closing down the factories. But I had no interest in an admin commission. I thought, *How am I in a position to be in charge of other girls who are probably all older than I am?* So I rejected that offer.

We had to take a bus to get to the Speke Ops Room, which was several miles away in Aughton Green in a little village school that had been evacuated. We were really in the country. In the summer we had the windows open. Occasionally a chicken would fly in through the window. One windy day a hay cart went by, and we had hay blowing into the Ops Room. When we had a break, we'd go out into the fields where the cows were, very bucolic but rather boring.

RAF Ops Room, World War II

The Speke fighter station was manned by three Polish squadrons. This was their rest area from the station north of London, Northolt. I thought, *Couldn't they send them a bit further north?* Because this was Liverpool, the area was very badly bombed. They were up all the time fighting, so that they had no more rest up in Lancashire than they had down in London. The Poles were great fighters.

Speke is where I learned to be a plotter and where I learned what the big secret was. We were getting plots from radar stations, and radar at that time was unknown to the general public. It was our secret weapon against the Germans. Before the war, the Germans had a dirigible that went patrolling out to the North Sea to try to find out what all these towers were that we were putting up along the east coast. Fortunately, at that time the towers weren't functioning, so the Germans didn't discover anything. But this was a big secret, why I couldn't tell my parents or anybody else what we were actually doing.

After a few months at Speke, I was itching to go where there was some action, so I kept applying to be posted back near London. Finally they said, "We will post you to Northolt," which is, of course, the other Polish fighter station near London. On the day I separated from Speke, I went to the airfield to await transportation to the train. When I got there they said, "You have to go down around the perimeter track of the airfield to that hut there. Take your kit with you." It had started to drizzle rain. My kit bag was heavy—had everything in it. I certainly couldn't put it over my shoulder as men did, so I had to drag it along. I was so embarrassed by all these Polish mechanics working on the fighters who were making sort of Polish remarks and whistling. When I got to the hut, I told them I was going to be stationed at Northolt. They said, "You must turn in your kit because you're getting a commission." I said, "I'm not getting a commission. I'm being reassigned to Northolt." They said, "Oh, somebody has made a mistake. That's the only reason to turn in your kit bag."

So I left, dragging my kit bag. On the way, an officer came along. I couldn't tell what rank he was because he was wearing a raincoat and a plastic cap over his hat. He said, "What are you doing in the rain with that kit bag?" And I said, "Oh, I'm being posted to Northolt, and for some reason they thought I was getting a commission." I was ranting and raving about the inefficiency of this airfield. He said, "Let's go back to my office, and I will get you transportation." I said, "Also, I'm afraid I'm going to miss my train to London." He said, "Oh, let's get out of the rain and I will arrange it for you." So he slung my kit bag over his shoulder and we went back. He showed me into his office and asked his secretary to bring me a cup of tea while he sought a mode of transportation. When she did I said, "What a nice man. Who is he?" She said, "Oh, he is the CEO of the station." I said, "Oh, oh, dear. I think I was a bit casual with him." She said, "Oh, he's a nice man. He won't mind." So she came back in again and said, "Your transportation is here." I didn't see him again to thank him, but I got down to London at last to Northolt.[1]

---

[1] RAF Northolt . . . is a Royal Air Force station in South Ruislip, 2 miles from Uxbridge in the London Borough of Hillingdon, West London. Approximately 6 mi north of London Heathrow Airport, the station also handles a large number of private civil flights. Northolt has one runway in operation, spanning 5,525 ft × 150 ft, with a grooved asphalt surface. Northolt pre-dates the establishment of the Royal Air Force by almost three years, having opened in May 1915. Originally established for the Royal Flying Corps, it has the longest history of continuous use of any RAF airfield. Before the outbreak of the Second World War, the station was the first to take delivery of the Hawker Hurricane. The station played a key role during the Battle of Britain, when fighters from several of its units, including No. 303 Polish Fighter Squadron, engaged enemy aircraft as part of the defense of London. It became the first base to have squadrons operating Supermarine Spitfire aircraft within German airspace. Source: http://en.wikipedia.org/wiki/RAF_Northolt, accessed May 27, 2013

Chapter Ten

NORTHOLT (1941), DANGEROUS MOONLIGHT, DENHAM FILM STUDIOS, KP DUTY

When I got to Northolt, we were billeted in quite a large house and we had our own recreation rooms. They provided a radio and a record player with records. Our Ops Room was in one of the shops in the town of Ruislip. In hot weather, we had the windows open and people outside could hear all of the instructions from the controller to the pilot, which was not too secretive to say the least. Also, we plotted air raids in different colors—red, yellow, blue—and changed the colors every five minutes. The plots on the wall were divided into segments so the controller would know how old the plots were for certain aircraft. Every time a train came into the station it somehow stopped the clock. So people would yell, "Red plots! We need more red plots!" Nobody had any left, then we'd realize the clock had stopped again. It finally sunk in that this was not a good place for the Ops Room to be.

So we relocated our Ops Room to a big house, which was owned by Sir John Anderson. Very pleasant surroundings. The Ops Room was attached to the house where the Polish controllers lived. Every hour we got a ten-minute break. Those who played tennis, when we stood down, would go out and play a game.

The Polish controllers were so jolly; laughing all the time, joking, and some of them were excellent piano players. They lived in another part of the house. In the summer they would have the French doors open and one of them would sit down to play Chopin or something at the piano. Then one of them said, "Ladies, you haven't heard anything yet!" He sort of flexed his one hand and fingers, then sat down and played chopsticks. He said, "That's my entire repertoire." We loved him. He only had one arm. Apparently he had been in a sortie over the channel. A shell had come through his cockpit and shot off his arm. It was lying in the bottom of the cockpit and, of course, he was bleeding profusely. He just managed to get back and land the plane before he passed out.

There were three Polish squadrons—302, 303 and 305—as far as I remember. They were very dashing, the pilot of 303 Squadron especially. They all had titles like baron or prince and had been weekend flyers before the war. Their jackets and greatcoats had red silk linings, and they wore white silk scarves—very dashing, indeed. Brilliant pilots. Their CO would make them go up between sorties and practice formation flying. They literally flew wingtip-to-wingtip. I felt so sorry for them because they had no idea of the fates of their families in occupied Poland. They were given nicknames to protect their families from reprisals by the Germans.[1]

---

[1] During the construction of Heathrow Airport, Northolt was used for commercial civil flights, becoming the busiest airport in Europe for a time and a major base for British European Airways. More recently the station has become the hub of British military flying operations in the London area. Northolt has been extensively redeveloped since 2006 to accommodate these changes, becoming home to the British Forces Post Office, which moved to a newly constructed headquarters and sorting office on the site. Units currently based at RAF Northolt are No. 32 (The Royal) Squadron, the Queen's Colour Squadron, 600 (City of London) Squadron, No 1 Aeronautical Information Documents Unit, the Air Historical Branch and the Central Band of the RAF. The station has also been used as a

About that time, a film called *Dangerous Moonlight* had been made about a Polish squadron in Warsaw as everything was falling around them. They were listening to the first notes of their national anthem on the radio. When that stopped, it meant that Poland had fallen. They had to get very beaten-up airplanes and fly them to England. The chief actor, Anton Walbrook, played one of the pilots who had been a composer in peacetime, so the theme music for the film was the Warsaw Concerto by Richard Addinsell. Even after the war it was a very popular concerto. In the last Winter Olympics [2010] they had a couple ice-skating to the Warsaw Concerto, although they referred to it as the Eagle Squadron.[2]

I think the mix-up there was because instead of the stitched wings that RAF pilots wore, the Polish pilots had silver eagles on a little chain, which was pinned to their breast pockets. But Eagle Squadron actually was a group of Americans who formed a squadron which flew with the RAF before America came into the war.

I remember ordering that record. In those days, a record would break if you dropped it. The very day I go to pick it up was the day when we had snow and ice. You had to tread very carefully because everywhere was just a thin layer of ice on the pavements and roads. I had to cross the road slipping and sliding, holding this record in its sleeve above my head. I wasn't going to break this record even if I fell and broke a leg. I took it back to our billet and everybody played it incessantly. I thought, they were going to wear the record out.

---

filming location for productions made at Pinewood Studios. Source: http://en.wikipedia.org/wiki/RAF_Northolt, June 9, 2013

2 *Dangerous Moonlight* (also known as *Suicide Squadron* in the USA) is a 1941 British film, starring Anton Walbrook, best known for its score written by Richard Addinsell with orchestrations by Roy Douglas, which includes the *Warsaw Concerto*. Among the costumes, the gowns were designed by Cecil Beaton. The film's love-story plot told mainly in flashbacks, revolves around the fictional composer of the *Warsaw Concerto*, a piano virtuoso and "shell-shocked" combat pilot, who meets an American war correspondent in Warsaw, and later returns from America to join the RAF in England to continue to fight against the Nazis and their occupation of Poland. Source: http://en.wikipedia.org/wiki/Dangerous_Moonlight, accessed April 19, 2013

Terry Smith World War II Ops Room sketches of plotters, telephonist, and controller.

The one great thing about being back in the London area was that Northolt was near Ruislip, another terminus for underground trains from central London. I had been starving for the theater, concerts, ballet and whatever since I was sent up north. So now on my days off, I could not only go home, although it was across London, but I could also in twenty minutes be in the theater district going to the theater. There was a group of Polish officers that another girl and I were talking to one day.

She was saying that the Polish ballet company had managed to escape to England, and were now performing in London. There were four officers, this girl and myself, and they said, "Well, when we're all off duty together, let's go up. We will take you to see this ballet." And it was wonderful because it was ballet I had never seen before. I had been so used to classical ballet, and here they were, beautiful dancers wearing their native costumes, which were very colorful. They did classic ballet, too, but what I really liked was that they were adapting their folk dances to ballet, and it was so exciting. That was one of the highlights of my time at Northolt.

We were also quite near the Denham Pinewood Studios, film studios. They were making a lot of patriotic films in those days, and when they wanted WAAF marching or WAAF doing something or the other, they would approach our station at Northolt. Usually it was one of the watches from the Ops Room who were not on duty that would be invited to go to be in one of the films. Of course, we were just background. We didn't get paid anything, but they arranged transport for us. It was interesting to go around; we had free range of what was going on in the film studios. They also gave us lunch, so, you know, it made a change. On one occasion they were making a movie called *Spitfire*. Leslie Howard [who portrayed Ashley Wilkes in *Gone With The Wind*] was in it. It was about the inventor of the Spitfire fighter plane named Reginald Mitchell and the story of his life. Leslie Howard was directing the movie as well. We had been asked to do a scene in the Operations Room.[3] So we sat around this table, plotting away at nothing in particular, but they made us wear navy blue overalls. We are not charwomen! Why are we wearing these overalls? Something to do with buttons on our uniforms being distracting in the lighting. So, to say the least, we were rather disgruntled. Our moment in the sun, so to speak, our

---

3 The studios were founded by Alexander Korda in 1935 on a 165 acre site near the village of Denham, Buckinghamshire. At the time it was the largest facility of its kind in the UK. In 1937, Queen Mary visited the studios while *The Drum* was being filmed. The studios were known by various names during their lifetime including London Film Studios, the home of Korda's London Films. It was merged with the Rank Organisation's Pinewood Studios to form D&P Studios; Pinewood is just 4 miles south of Denham. Film makers were said to prefer Denham as a location, leading to Pinewood Studios being used for storage during the Second World War. Some of the notable films made at Denham include, *The Thief of Baghdad*, *49th Parallel*, *Brief Encounter*, *Great Expectations*, *Hamlet*. Bernard Miles said that "when the technicians, the electricians and carpenters and so on, on the floor, who had been watching a scene filmed, applauded, you knew it was good, because they'd seen the best." Colin Sorensen, who as a schoolboy often used to watch the work going on at Denham recalled the sight "of the main studio buildings, a great mass of, probably asbestos, grey-green roofs" and the smell of "cellulose paint merged with newly cut soft wood." The proximity of Denham Aerodrome was sometimes problematic. Mary Morris remembered that an intimate scene with Leslie Howard, for *Pimpernel Smith* was "interrupted 22 times by aircraft noise." Denham's final film was made in 1952, and the J. Arthur Rank Company went on to rent the facility to the United States Air Force between 1955 and December 1961. In the 1960s and 70s Rank Xerox occupied the Art Deco office buildings and used most of the sound stages as warehouses. The buildings were demolished in 1981 and the site re-landscaped as a business park. Source: https://en.wikipedia.org/wiki/Denham_Film_Studios, accessed May 27, 2013

seconds of fame, and we were wearing these drab navy overalls. The scene was short. It was just this controller, who actually was an actor in peacetime named Sir Raymond whom I had seen in a lot of B movies, as the 'head controller'. I guess Leslie Howard, out of sight of the camera on the other side, directed the scene as to appear a bomb was to have fallen nearby. Everybody ducked down, and Sir Raymond said, "That was a near one," to whoever he was speaking to on the phone. I can't believe that it took an hour just to do that one sentence because the lighting wasn't right or the sound wasn't right. No wonder they cost so much to produce. I have a DVD of that film and I can't tell who is who. We all look the same. The children would say to me, "Which one is you?" I would say, "I don't know. We all look alike," because we would take a break and leave, and afterwards we wouldn't all go back to the same place. We would go back to the nearest one to us. We kept moving around, so I don't know which one was me, but that was my two seconds of fame.

About a week later, who should come in the Ops Room but this Sir Raymond who played the controller, still in this uniform with the wings. We thought, *What's he come here for when we've already done the Ops Room scene.* So he came, sat with the Polish controllers and was chatting away with them. After he left we asked one of the Poles, "Who is he? I mean, we know who he is. He's an actor, but why is he here?" He said, "He was a fighter pilot in World War I. He's reenlisted, and now he's our chief controller." So life imitates the film in some way.

We also had several actors and actresses who patriotically joined the service but were strategically stationed near the Pinewood and Dehnam Film Studios so that they could do their little bits of being on film. We had a little room off the main Ops Room. I can't remember what we were supposed to be doing in there, but there were four of us. One of them was Michael Hammond, and we asked each other what they did in civilian life. He said,

"I was an actor." Someone said, "Oh, really. What was the latest film you were in?" He said, "I was in *Things to Come*, that H. G. Wells movie." So we said, "Oh, what part did you play?" He said, "I was put in a rocket with a girl and we were shot to the moon to populate it." Well, everybody else roared with laughter. I knew that he was a little a little effeminate, but I didn't know why everybody roared with laughter until two years later. I had never heard of homosexuals or gays. I think they were called gay at that time, and so I didn't know what they were talking about.

About a year later, I was walking down Bond Street when here comes a vision of Michael Hammond in an officer's uniform. I liked Michael, but he didn't have a lot up in the attic, so to speak. But here he was with a commission. So we stopped and spoke. I said, "Congratulations on your commission. What is it in?" He said, "Now, darling, don't laugh. It's in intelligence." Well, I didn't laugh, but I did think, *Well, there goes the war. Bless his heart.*

That same day, I went to Fortnum & Mason, a department store, to have coffee, and who should come in but Noni Spencer Green who I had known up in Lancashire when we were stationed at Aughton Springs. She said, "Hello, fellow felon!" I said, "Were we felons?" She said, "Don't you remember on our day off we decided to go into the big seaside town of Southport, and we walked along the country lane to catch a single-decker bus that came along about every other hour. We stood waiting about 15 minutes when along comes a Black Maria [police van] that was transporting prisoners? The policeman got out, came to us and said, 'What are you standing here for?' We said, 'We're waiting for the bus.' He said, 'Oh, it's a long drive. You'll have another hour and a half to wait. You better hop in. We will give you a lift.' We said, 'Will you get us to Southport?' and he said, 'Yes, we will give you a lift there.' We looked very apprehensive, so he said, 'It's all right we don't have any prisoners in there.'

"So we climbed in the back of the Black Maria, and we were hoping that when they got to Southport they would stop at a discreet distance from the sea front and deposit us on a side street, but much to our embarrassment they drove right along the sea front and parked and came around and opened the doors. A cluster of people surrounded us to see what felons were getting out of this Black Maria. It was we two little WAAFs. So we made a great show thanking them so much for giving us this lift."

We had an enjoyable afternoon there, catching the right bus this time. When we got back, to our consternation, we found that we were supposed to be on fire duty, and apparently somebody had forgotten to tell us. So they said, "Oh, well, you'll have to do KP for an hour tomorrow," because it was too late that night. The next day we were on duty in the morning, so in the afternoon we toddled along to the kitchen and told the cook that we had been put on KP for an hour. She said, "What can you do in the kitchen?" We looked at each other and told her not very much. Neither of us had been near kitchens on a regular basis. "So what can you do? Do you know anything about cooking?" "No." "Well, let me see. I think the safest thing to give you to do is to peel potatoes. Can't do much harm there."

Neither of us knew how to peel potatoes either. We stood at the sink and hacked away at these potatoes. The cook eventually rushed up and said, "Stop! At this rate we won't have any potatoes left for dinner." Noni said, "Look, if we give one of your assistants half a crown each," (which was about 30 cents) "would they peel the potatoes for us?" And so two of them leapt eagerly at the chance. Now 30 cents doesn't seem worthwhile peeling potatoes, but back in 1941, you could buy a good dinner for half a crown. They started peeling potatoes, and the cook said, "But you haven't been here for an hour. You have to stay the rest of the hour." So we sat on a table singing musical songs like "She Was Only a Bird in a Beautiful Cage" and, "Yes, We Have No Bananas," Eventually everybody started singing along with us. We had a good old sing-song. At the end of the hour, we jumped down and said, "Well, nice to know you. Goodbye." The cook said, "Thank you very much for coming," and they looked a little disappointed that we weren't going to go on sort of cheering them on with our songs. As we left, the cook said, "Good-bye you lovely luscious lumps of lure." We looked at each other, "Lovely luscious lumps of lure?" Well, unfortunately, this got out to the rest of our watch.

One day I had occasion to go out to the station headquarters where the airfield was. As I walked to the station at HQ, I was passing the airfield. One of the Spitfires came in on a very wobbly course, made a very wobbly landing, sort of drifted off the runway, ran into a hedge and then stopped. The black wagon and the fire engine dashed out there. I stopped to see what had happened. They opened the cockpit, and there was the pilot, fast asleep. He had just come back from a sortie, had probably been out before then and was just completely exhausted. He just had managed to land the plane back on the airfield.

When I came out of the HQ, it had started to rain and they were about to take the flag down. I tried to sneak past so I didn't have to stand in the rain and salute the flag. But I got a baleful look from the officer in charge, so I stood there and got soaking wet while I royally saluted the flag as it was lowered.

I have to say I really admired the Polish pilots stationed there so much. They had been through so much in their own country. They had to leave their families behind not knowing what had happened to them after Germans overtook Poland. I heard all the horrible tales; not the least were the terrible prison camps, especially the treatment of Jewish people there. But they always seemed so cheerful; hiding their sorrow very well. They were tenacious pilots.

They used to go up practicing formation flying when they weren't actually going on sorties, and they would fly wing tip to wing tip. I don't know how they did that, but I really admired them very much.

About that time, my sister Sylvia and Angus married. He took an intelligence course and eventually went to Bletchley Park where they cracked the German code (which contributed to the war effort very much). Sylvia joined the foreign office and became a political intelligence officer. I don't know how she got into Intelligence. We didn't discuss those things because we saw each other so rarely during the war. We didn't talk about what we did.[4]

Once when I went on 24-hour leave while I was stationed at Northolt, I visited my parents in their flat overlooking the Thames

---

4 The Enigma cypher was the backbone of German military and intelligence communications. Invented in 1918, it was initially designed to secure banking communications, but achieved little success in that sphere. The German military, however, were quick to see its potential. They thought it to be unbreakable, and not without good reason. Enigma's complexity was bewildering. The odds against anyone who did not know the settings being able to break Enigma were a staggering 150 million to one. The Poles had broken Enigma in 1932, when the encoding machine was undergoing trials with the German Army. They even managed to reconstruct a machine. At that time, the cypher altered only once every few months. With the advent of war, it changed at least once a day, effectively locking the Poles out. But in July 1939, they had passed on their knowledge to the British and the French. This enabled the code breakers to make critical progress in working out the order in which the keys were attached to the electrical circuits, a task that had been impossible without an Enigma machine in front of them. Armed with this knowledge, the code breakers were then able to exploit a chink in Enigma's armor. A fundamental design flaw meant that no letter could ever be encrypted as itself; an A in the original message, for example, could never appear as an A in the code. This gave the code breakers a toehold. Errors in messages sent by tired, stressed or lazy German operators also gave clues. In January 1940 came the first break into Enigma. It was in Huts 3, 6, 4 and 8 that the highly effective Enigma decrypt teams worked. The huts operated in pairs and, for security reasons, were known only by their numbers. The code breakers concentrating on the Army and Air Force cyphers were based in Hut 6, supported by a team in the neighboring Hut 3 who turned the deciphered messages into intelligence reports. Hut 8 decoded messages from the German Navy, with Hut 4 the associated naval intelligence hut. Their raw material came from the 'Y' Stations: a web of wireless intercept stations dotted around Britain and in a number of countries overseas. These stations listened in to the enemy's radio messages and sent them to Bletchley Park to be decoded and analyzed. To speed up the code breaking process, the brilliant mathematician Alan Turing developed an idea originally proposed by Polish cryptanalysts. The result was the Bombe: an electro-mechanical machine that greatly reduced the odds, and thereby the time required, to break the daily-changing Enigma keys. Source: http://www.bletchleypark.org.uk/content/hist/wartime.rhtm, accessed April 19, 2013

in Surbiton. My father was out somewhere for the day and Mother was still working for the WVS. She wanted me to type a letter for her, and, unthinkingly, I said, "I'm so sorry. I don't know how to type." She looked at me in amazement and said, "You have been in the WAAF two years and you haven't learned to type yet? No wonder you don't have a commission." I had to bite my tongue, look humble and stupid, because I couldn't tell her or my father what I actually did. They thought I was just a rather pathetic clerk who hadn't learned to type yet.

Although I was offered a commission in administration five weeks after I joined the service when I was 17, it dawned on me that the only officers in the control rooms, in the Ops Rooms, were ex-air crew. So unless you were ex-air crew, you couldn't get a commission in your field, which was very frustrating.

Chapter Eleven

UXBRIDGE (1942)

About this time, I was posted to 11 Group Headquarter in Uxbridge on the outskirts of north London. Uxbridge was of strategic importance, especially during the Battle of Britain, because it covered the southeast corner of Britain where most of the action took place at that time. Our Ops Room was about 80 feet underground. We had air conditioning pumped in there through vents. We were told we wouldn't be gassed at all if we were so far below ground. However, this was a very low-lying area and we used to get a lot of fog. It would come drifting through our vents, even though we were that far below ground. I thought, *Well, if the fog can come through the vents, I would imagine that gas could come through the vents, too.* Once we had an air raid, and a bomb fell on the water main. We were sloshing around on the floor of the Operations Room ankle deep in water.

Our CO of the Ops Room, Mallory, had a brother, George, who was the one who climbed Everest. As we were near the Pinewood and Denham Film Studios, we had actors there, too. One of them was David Niven who was representing the army; had joined a Scottish regiment. They wore kilts and were very dashing. Another one was Rex Harrison, who I think had something to do with flying control. He was in one of the glass booths overlooking the floor, and periodically he would dive behind the desk. We concluded he liked his tipple [alcohol], so it was quite an interesting time there.

Restored Operations Room in underground bunker at RAF Uxbridge. Map (table) and plotter (mannequin, left), with RAF Station names and readiness status boards on wall.

I remember once going on duty and David Niven was just coming off duty. He stopped me and said, "This isn't a line, but I'm sure I've seen you before somewhere." I said, "Well, you did nearly knock me over on Guilford High Street a couple years ago." I had been shopping. He had come out of a newsstand reading a paper and walked straight into me. He said, "Oh, my gosh, are you all right?" And I said, "Yes, I'm fine, thank you." He looked so concerned, bless his heart. That was quite interesting, although I didn't enjoy being that far underground. We had a lot of visitors like Winston Churchill and other members of Parliament who came to see what was going on.

While I was at 11 Group Headquarters, they asked for six volunteers to go on something very hush-hush down in Sussex. I thought, *This sounds like just the job for me.* Mother had been urging me to get a commission, and I knew I didn't want anything in admin or pay accounts or equipment. She thought all during the war that I was a filing clerk, since I told her I was Clerk, Special Duties—couldn't tell anybody what I did. I thought maybe I would be able to get a commission in code and cipher. I applied for that and was told they were only training men to go overseas in that capacity at that time and that I should apply again in six months. I thought that meanwhile I'd volunteer and see what this hush-hush project was.

While waiting to go to Tangmere, I was assigned to the Ops Room at Durrington, which had been built so hastily underground that after a few months one side of the building started to sink sideways, which made it impossible for us to do any plotting because the plots or all the paraphernalia just slid off the table. They had to abandon that Ops Room.

Soon, six of us proceeded down to Chichister, the nearest town to Tangmere, the Number 1 fighter station in England.

Chapter Twelve

TANGMERE (1942), DOUG BADER

When we got to Tangmere and reported to station headquarters, they said they had no idea why we were there or what this secret unit was going to be. While they found out they told us, "Well, you better go and stay at Fontwell," which in peacetime was a horse racecourse. It was about ten miles outside Chichester, which was the town nearest to Tangmere. We went out to this place and were put in the tearoom. There were about half a dozen of us. We were assigned these cots where normally they would have a table for people to eat on. For our ablutions we had to go over to the jockeys' area to do our washing, showers and et cetera there. There was no racing during World War II, so it was just completely empty, but it was very nice. It was summertime. There was a sunken garden and, on Sundays, we would sit out there and sun. For meals, we had to walk quite a long way up to an estate where pay accounts [payroll] had moved to. To have meals, we had to eat there, which was quite boring to have to walk all that way for an indifferent meal and walk all the way back again.[1]

---

1 RAF Tangmere was a Royal Air Force station famous for its role in the Battle of Britain, located at Tangmere village about 3 miles (5 km) east of Chichester in West Sussex, England. American RAF pilot Billy Fiske died at Tangmere and was the first American aviator to die

HER FINEST HOUR

We really got fed up with this after several weeks, so we all piled on the local bus and went back to Tangmere again and said, "Look, we've got to do something. We're just sitting here twiddling our thumbs." Our superiors said, "Well, why would you want to deliberately look for something? Can't you enjoy having a little vacation?" We said, "Not when everybody else is having to do something for our country." They said the hush-hush project hadn't been set up yet, but they would absorb us into the Ops Room at Tangmere, which wasn't what we were looking forward to doing. We were billeted in Bishop Otter College in Chichester and had to walk to the Ops Room, which had been a kindergarten school with pint-sized bathroom facilities. The assembly hall was the Ops Room.

One day I was up at SHQ [Station Headquarters] trying to open a door. It seemed to be stuck, so I kept tugging at it. Suddenly it

---

during World War II. Famous World War II ace Douglas Bader was a Wing Commander at Tangmere in 1941.... As war threatened in the late thirties, the fighters became faster, with Hawker Furies, Gloster Gladiators, and the Hawker Hurricanes powered by the famous Merlin engines all being used at Tangmere. In 1939 the airfield was enlarged to defend the south coast against attack by the Luftwaffe, with Tangmere's only hotel and some houses being demolished in the process. The RAF commandeered the majority of houses in the center of the village, with only six to eight families being allowed to stay. It was only in 1966 that the village resumed its status as a civilian community. In August 1940 the first squadron (No. 602 Squadron RAF) of Supermarine Spitfires was based at the satellite airfield at nearby Westhampnett, as the Battle of Britain began. By now the villagers had mainly been evacuated, and extensive ranges of RAF buildings had sprung up. The first and worst enemy raid on the station came on 16 August 1940 when hundreds of Stuka dive bombers and fighters crossed the English coast and most headed for Tangmere. Soon, the Stukas started to dive on Tangmere, there was extensive damage to buildings and aircraft on the ground and 14 ground staff and six civilians were killed, but the station was kept in service and brought back into full operation. Throughout the war, the station was also a secret base for the Special Operations Executive who flew agents in and out of occupied France to strengthen the Resistance. The SOE used Tangmere Cottage, opposite the main entrance to the base. Today the cottage sports a commemorative plaque to its former secret life. Later in the war, as the RAF turned from defence to attack, the legendary Group Captain Douglas Bader—the legless fighter ace—commanded the Tangmere wing of Fighter Command. Today he is commemorated in the *Bader Arms* public house in the village. Many of those killed at the base, from both sides in conflict, are buried in the cemetery at St Andrews Church, Tangmere; today tended by the Commonwealth War Graves Commission. Source: http://en.wikipedia.org/wiki/RAF_Tangmere, accessed June 1, 2013

jerked open, and Dougie [Douglas] Bader was on the other side. He had been trying to open the door, too. We were in a tug-of-war, and he sort of fell in on top of me. Thank goodness he didn't fall over, because it would have been difficult to help someone up who had artificial legs.

Doug Bader was the CO of a squadron at Tangmere. He had lost both of his legs in a pre-war accident. He flew Spitfires but was eventually shot down over France. When he bailed out of the plane in a parachute, one of the artificial legs crumpled on impact. He was taken prisoner, and it was arranged by the Germans to allow a lone RAF plane to fly over and drop a replacement leg for him, which was done. But, of course, he tried to escape, so his legs were taken away from him at night.[2]

---

2 Group Captain Sir Douglas Robert Steuart Bader (pron.: /'bɑ:dər/), CBE, DSO & Bar, DFC & Bar, FRAeS, DL (21 February 1910–5 September 1982) was a Royal Air Force (RAF) fighter ace during the Second World War. He was credited with 20 aerial victories, four shared victories, six probables, one shared probable and 11 enemy aircraft damaged. Bader joined the RAF in 1928, and was commissioned in 1930. In December 1931, while attempting some aerobatics, he crashed and lost both his legs. Having been on the brink of death, he recovered, retook flight training, passed his check flights and then requested reactivation as a pilot. Although there were no regulations applicable to his situation, he was retired on medical grounds. After the outbreak of the Second World War in 1939, however, Bader returned to the RAF and was accepted as a pilot. He scored his first victories over Dunkirk during the Battle of France in 1940. He then took part in the Battle of Britain and became a friend and supporter of Air Vice-Marshal Trafford Leigh-Mallory and his "Big Wing" experiments. In August 1941, Bader bailed out over German-occupied France and was captured. Soon afterward, he met and befriended Adolf Galland, a prominent German fighter ace. The circumstances surrounding how Bader was shot down in 1941 are controversial. Recent research strongly suggests he was a victim of friendly fire. Despite his disability, Bader made a number of escape attempts and was eventually sent to the POW camp at Colditz Castle. He remained there until April 1945 when the camp was liberated by the First United States Army. Bader left the RAF permanently in February 1946 and resumed his career in the oil industry. During the 1950s, a book and a film, *Reach for the Sky*, chronicled his life and RAF career to the end of the Second World War. Bader campaigned for the disabled—for which he was knighted in 1976—and continued to fly until ill health forced him to stop in 1979. Three years later, at the age of 72, Bader died on 5 September 1982, from a sudden heart attack. Source: http://en.wikipedia.org/wiki/Douglas_Bader, accessed April 28, 2013

Douglas Bader

In the same squadron was a young man called Colin Hodgkinson who had lost his legs when he was 17 in a flying accident in the war. He was also shot down and made a prisoner of war. One didn't hear much about Colin because Doug Bader was a CO and got all the glory. I knew Colin. He was a friend of a friend of mine, Noni Spencer Greene, whom I had met at Speke. He would insist on dancing with her, although it was agony for him to do so. The perspiration would pour down his face. She said it was something his ego required him to do, but it was painful to watch him dance. Another person I met at Tangmere was Joan Cheesewright, who has remained my friend all these years. She was also in Ops.

One day I was invited to have tea with a Naval officer. We went to one of these rickety little old Georgian houses on the high street. A Luftwaffe tip-and-run raid came over and dropped bombs. We were in a tiny room upstairs, crowded with people, and we all tried to dive under the tables. He and two other girls were under the table, and there was no room for me, so I just turned sideways in my chair and kept my head down. The whole building shook. This Naval office got up afterwards, red in the face, and said, "Why didn't you get down on the floor?" I said, "You took up all the room under there." If that was going to be a budding romance, it ended right there.

There were four watches in the Ops Room at Tangmere, which meant there were about 50 or 60 girls. The administrative staff resented us because we all seemed to be off-duty. Either one watch would be coming off duty, another resting, or another watch about to come on duty, another watch might be off for 24 hours. So there always seemed to be a lot of us around doing nothing. We escaped all the usual duties other girls had to do because we worked shift hours.

One day, I was about to go on duty. It had been raining, when I came out of the mess hall, my shoe slipped on a manhole. I went down on my side and broke my arm. One of the WAFF went back to my room while I changed my stockings, which was not easy with a broken arm because back then we didn't have tights [panty hoses]. The stockings had suspender belts. But I still had to go on duty, so they put me on the teleprinter. As the evening wore on it became harder to hold onto anything. The next morning, I had to have someone help me dress because we had collars that were separate from our shirts, and I had to have my tie tied for me. I went to the hospital, but had to wait until I finally nabbed the first doctor who walked by and told him, "Look here, I broke my arm 24 hours ago and I would like someone to set it." He said, "Oh my poor, girl. Come with me." Eventually, I did get it set. Boy, if you don't have a commission, it's hard to get anything done in the Air Force.

Tangmere was such a big complex that we had satellite stations—airfields—around the area. When I was getting promoted to the next level, I had to take an oral exam and was not allowed to write anything down in preparation because it might fall into the wrong hands. One of the things I had to learn was all of the call signs of the squadrons and which airfield they were. Every time I went on duty I would memorize them during a lull. The day before the exam an airman came in and changed all the calls signs, so I had to memorize them all over again... overnight. Somehow I passed the exam. At Christmas, our watch put on a show. One of our songs was directed to Lord Dudley, the CO. It went something like:

Oh, dear Lord Dudley
Oh, dear Lord Dudley
With your little dachshund, Dennis
We think you are so cuddly

This was quite a stretch of imagination, because he was very austere man and rarely smiled; not one you associate with being a cuddly person. However, it was the only word we could rhyme with Dudley.

After what seemed like endless waiting, the six of us who had come to Tangmere from Uxbridge were finally told that systems were all go for the "hush-hush" project. They said, "You will report to Southampton and board a ferry to take you to the Isle of Wight. You will get on the bus that will take you to the southern tip of the island to a place called Niton Undercliff. An officer will meet you when you get off the bus. There you will report to duty."

Chapter Thirteen

ISLE OF WIGHT, BLACKGANG (1943), THE MILK RUN, MINEFIELD, MICHAEL CUDDON, DEATH RAY

When our superior told us to catch "the bus," we concluded that there was only one bus a day that struggled across the island. When we got to Cowes [Isle of Wight], we finally found a single-decker bus and loaded ourselves on it accompanied by country people carrying baskets of eggs, chickens, and, at one point, we had a pig on board. We stopped at every bus stop all the way across the island. It was like stepping back in time.

The officer was, indeed, there to meet us at Niton Undercliff. He showed us where we would be billeted, which was with village residents who had rooms to spare. Then we were told to report to duty at the Buddle Inn, which was next door to the house where another girl and I were staying. We were told that in the time of Napoleon and the wars, smugglers used to roll barrels of brandy or ale or whatever from France. They would roll them up the cliff to the Buddle Inn, which is still there. Incidentally, our call sign was Blackgang, I suppose after the "Blackgang Chine" smugglers in Napoleon's time.[1,2]

So we reported to the inn and were led up a long cliff until we came to the top where we were met by a guard who opened a gate that led us in to a field of cows. We looked at each other and said, "This is our special project?"

At the far end of the field was a trailer. In front of the trailer was what looked like a hut on top of a turntable with an antenna on top. There was another trailer at the opposite end of the field. The

---

1 In Hampshire, the smuggler's job was made especially easy by the proximity of the Isle of Wight. The island had a well-developed trade in wool exports, and until the late 18th century, its coasts were only lightly guarded against the attentions of free-traders [smugglers]: any ship's master with sufficient navigational ability would have been able to slip into one of the island's bays or creeks with little risk of losing a cargo to the land-based forces.... the free-trade apparently enjoyed the support of many of the inhabitants. To a certain extent this may reflect the fact that many local people despised rule from the mainland—until the end of the 13th century Wight had been an independent principality, and even at this early date, export smuggling of wool was already taking place on the island and the mainland.... When the chance of detection was slight, most free-traders preferred to land goods on the south-west coast of the island. Here there are a few more accessible landing points than the south-east, and they were all pushed into use: notable landing points were Blackgang Chine, Walpan, Ladder, Branes, Grange, Chilton, Brook, Shippard's and Compton Chines, Freshwater Bay and Scratchell's Bay. The chines in particular were valuable points of entry, because most featured a safe beach on the coast, and a secure path inland, hidden from view by dense brushwood and small trees. Source: http://www.smuggling.co.uk/gazetteer_s_10.html, accessed April 22, 2013

2 Blackgang is a village on the south coast of the Isle of Wight. It is best known as the location of the Blackgang Chine amusement park which sits to the south of St Catherine's Down. Blackgang forms the west end of the Ventnor Undercliff region, which extends for 12 kilometers from Blackgang to Luccombe, also encompassing the town of Ventnor and the villages of Bonchurch, St Lawrence, and Niton. It also marks the edge of the Back of the Wight. There is some concern that the Ventnor Undercliff area is experiencing substantial coastal erosion. Historically, Blackgang was the location of a major chine, the coastal ravine after which the Blackgang Chine Park was named; this was obliterated by landslides and coastal erosion over the 20th century. It is historically known for being a haunt of smugglers. The nearby Sandrock Spring, a Chalybeate spring, was discovered in 1811. This too was destroyed in a landslide in 1978. Clifftop walks in and around the area give panoramic views of the English Channel and the south-western Isle of Wight coast (the Back of the Wight). Blackgang is also notable for dinosaur fossils (see Dinosaurs of the Isle of Wight) and the nudist Blackgang Beach. Source: http://en.wikipedia.org/wiki/Blackgang, accessed April 22, 2013

Blackgang (left), Niton Undercliff (right), Isle of Wight

officer said, "This is GCI—Ground Control Interception. We are the nearest radar station to the French coast. Along the road is a town called Ventnor. The RAF has an underground RDF [Radio Direction Finder], which tracks bombers and other planes."

The Germans had a habit of flying early in the morning under Ventnor's radar through the mist. It was called "The Milk Run"; always over the channel in the morning. Our job was to pick up planes that were under Ventnor's radar. We were a GCI station, which meant we could monitor planes coming under the radar almost at sea level.

The officer told us, "Ventnor has tip-and-run raiders who try to bomb them. When we start operating, the Germans will turn their attention on us as well."

I said, "Where do we take cover?" He said, "Underneath the trailer." I said, "Isn't that where they will be aiming?" He said, "Do you have a better idea?" I thought, "Where have I heard that before?" I looked around this field, which had no trees or any other cover except to the cows, and I didn't fancy trusting my luck to having a cow fall on top of me. I said, "I guess this will have to do."

We soon set up operation and got things going. At that time, in the infant stages of radar, the aerial was manually controlled. Some poor young man sat in the antenna hut. When the controller pressed a button, he turned the antenna one way, and when the controller pressed another button, he turned the antenna another direction. One day when we stood down, we were talking with a young man who had been a flight sergeant and had been grounded for some reason. He was absolutely furious at being stationed there, I could sympathize with him. He had to sit in a dark little hut just obeying signal from our controller in our trailer. That was what he had been reduced to.

This was the way they made radar sweeps. Inside the control room, we would see a wand move around a screen picking up blips that represented planes in combat. One of the blips would be an enemy plane, and one would be our fighter. When they were mixing it up, you couldn't tell which plane was which. The controller would say to our pilot, "Let your canary sing," and the pilot would send a signal from his plane. When that happened, another little blip would come out of one of the blips. That way, we could identify which plane was ours.

At night, the pilots had no means of seeing the enemy, so they relied on the radar controller putting them onto the target. We had what we called the "Y" service, which would report to us the instructions the German controller had given his pilot. Unfortunately, the Germans also had the equivalent service, which relayed the instructions our controllers gave to our pilots. So it was matter of who got the instructions first.

There were six positions inside the control room. We all sat around a central radar area. The position I liked best was the one where I sat a lighted desk with a map of the area we covered which was covered with a plastic-like sheet. My job was to record with a chinagraph [grease] pencil the time of the plots of each aircraft as I got the instructions from the controller, so that when they had a postmortem afterwards up at fighter command, they would know exactly what the maneuvers were and at what times.

That position and the one at the telephone desk were the only lighted places in the room. We were in complete darkness otherwise, except for the light from the radar screen. After doing this for an hour or two, it became quite a strain on the eyes. After several months, it started to affect my eyesight.

When we stood down we could rest in the other trailer at the other side of the field. If the bell sounded, we had to be across the field and operating our sets within three minutes, which could be challenging at night because one would not only encounter cows but their calling cards as well.

In the area we were operating were commandos who spoke French. They might have been Bretons—a fearsome lot with daggers who seemed to be a law unto themselves. Locals shrank away from them. We heard that they used to practice garroting [strangling] sentries by garroting the local sheep or pigs, which the farmers protested very loudly about to the government.

One day another WAAF and I decided to explore the surroundings. We went through the little village of Niton Undercliff, wandered around and found some other interesting places. On the way back, we said, "Oh, we've got to go all the way back through the village and up to where we were billeted. Let's take a shortcut and go through these woods. We will come out on the coast road. It won't be too far from where we live." So we went through the woods and came across this field, and, to our alarm when we got to the end of the field, there was barbed wire all along a bank on the edge of the field. Down below was the coast road. We were in a dilemma. I said, "Well, we will just have to go back, I guess, take the long way around." The other girl said, "Wait a minute. What's this sign here say?" So we peered around to it because it was facing the road. There were skull and cross bones at the top and it said, "Beware. Land Mine Field." I don't know what guardian angels were watching us as we walked across this land mine field, that we weren't blown up, but we realized we couldn't possibly go across the field again. Our luck wouldn't hold out twice, but neither could we get over this roll of barbed wire.

Presently we heard the tramping march of feet and thought, *Saved at last!* We had mixed feelings when along came this unit of commandos from the very tough looking young men who we all avoided. They came clomping around the road in sort of a disarray of clothes, which was supposed to be some sort of uniform. The officer halted them, saw our dilemma, and they threw their rain Macs [Macintosh, a waterproof raincoat] over the barbed wire and told us to climb over it. They caught us before we fell to the ground from that height. We were very grateful to them. But at other times we all avoided them. They clomped around with knives in their stockings. I mean, they didn't wear uniforms at all because they were commandos. They were very fierce young men, but they did save us that day.

It was estimated that, in an invasion, the Isle of Wight would be one of the first places attacked by the Germans, so we had to learn to throw a mills bomb [hand grenade], use a rifle and a Sten gun [9 mm submachine gun], and learn how to dismantle the radar station so that it could not be used if it fell into enemy hands. We weren't individually issued with these weapons of war, but they were in the control room. Can you imagine the German army landing on Niton Undercliff? We little WAAF would stand there with our Sten guns and repel the whole German army? Ha, ha.

We were also required to man a naval radar site, which was a little further up the cliff. This was to sweep for enemy small craft or boats that might be making their way towards us from France. It was very uncomfortable one night when we plotted German E boats that came right up under our cliff. We were hoping and praying that they wouldn't realize that all around England they had put land mines and barbed wire on the coast, but they had cleared our little cove so that we and a nearby Hampshire regiment could use it to bathe and swim. The Germans could have gone back and said, "Oh, there's a place that we can just waltz right in." We were very pleased to have that cove. That's where I met Michael.³

Another time, a group of us went down to the coast to sunbathe and swim. There was really only room for one person on this very narrow path. As we were coming back up, we passed a group of young officers from the Hampshire regiment going down the path to the beach.

We all had to walk sideways so we could pass one another. One of them came eye-to-eye with me. I felt an immediate attraction to him, which was very strange because I had been reticent about conversing with them. We sort of nodded to each other, but that's where I first saw Michael Cuddon, my fiancée. I had never dated anybody before, even though I was 18 or 19 at time, but we were immediately attracted to each other for some reason. I thought he was outstanding.

---

3 E-boats (German: *Schnellboot*, or *S-Boot*, meaning "fast boat") was the designation for fast attack craft of the Kriegsmarine during World War II. It is commonly held that the British used the term *E* for *Enemy*. Source: http://en.wikipedia.org/wiki/E-boat, April 22, 2013

About a week later, they had a party at their officers' club and invited us to go along. I met Michael again. The others were rollicking around, and we just sat to one side and found we had so much in common like the love of the theatre, reading and music. He was very quiet, but had a great sense of humor. I really enjoyed his company. He said, "I find it so difficult to talk to girls who aren't interested in the things I'm interested in." I said, "I have found exactly the same thing." We got to know each other very well, so that started a fine romance for us.

One day two elderly ladies came up to the gate with baskets and told the guard, "We have come to pick mushrooms." He said, "I'm sorry. This is a restricted area. You can't come in here." They were highly indignant. "But we've been picking mushrooms here since we were little girls!" They just couldn't understand it at all and were really very annoyed that they were turned away.

One night the NCO was swiveling the antenna around as the controller instructed. The door to the hut flew open, but he couldn't get up to close it. The next morning a delegation came up from the village of Niton Undercliff and told the guard at the gate that they wished to speak to the officer in charge. So the officer in charge came down, and the head of the delegation said, "With great respect, we would appreciate it in the future if your death ray would not sweep over our village!" Of course, the officer was taken aback that they thought we were operating a death ray. He had to think quickly because he couldn't tell them what we were doing, so he said, "Oh, we were experimenting with a new sort of search light. Sorry if it came in your direction." I never heard of an oblong searchlight, but it seemed to satisfy them.

As we were the radar station for Tangmere, they decided we should have some protection from tip-and-run raids. One morning at dawn they sent a Spitfire to patrol the area between Ventnor and Blackgang. I was just going on duty to relieve the night crew and reached the cliff when I saw the Spitfire. At the same time, out of the ocean mist, came a Messerschmitt. The Spitfire went after him. Tangmere sent another Spitfire to assist. They were having this mix-up almost at sea level, and as the radar station was on a cliff, I was looking right out at them. This was an exciting moment to see a dog fight taking place in front of my eyes. The Spitfires chased the Messerschmitt out to sea. The last I saw of them, all three planes were tearing off into the distance in the mist.

I can't remember how many months I was stationed there. The days sort of ran together because no church bells were allowed to ring unless there was an air raid. I do know that the radar work was affecting my eyes. I was also informed that the next batch of officer cadets would begin training for code and cipher commissions. I thought I needed to go back to the mainland and get ready for that. So I went back to Tangmere. When I was reassigned to the mainland, I went with much regret because I wouldn't see Michael as much, but we wrote to each other.

Chapter Fourteen

RETURN TO TANGMERE, CHANEL NO. 5, ENGAGEMENT, MICHAEL'S DEATH

Tangmere was the biggest fighter station in Britain and had satellite stations all around Appledram and Westhampnett with a night fighter station at Ford and an air-sea rescue at Shoreham along the coast. Ford had twin-engine Mosquito fighter-bombers that would go over the Channel at night. About that time they had made Ford a Number 1 night fighter station, which meant it had the facilities to deal with any type of aircraft, be it fighter or bomber.[1]

---

[1] The de Havilland DH.98 Mosquito was a British multi-role combat aircraft, with a two-man crew, that served during the Second World War and the postwar era. The Mosquito was one of the few operational, front-line aircraft of the World War II era to be constructed almost entirely of wood and, as such, was nicknamed "The Wooden Wonder". The Mosquito was also known affectionately as the "Mossie" to its crews. Originally conceived as an unarmed fast bomber, the Mosquito was adapted to many other roles during the air war, including: low- to medium-altitude daytime tactical bomber, high-altitude night bomber, pathfinder, day or night fighter, fighter-bomber, intruder, maritime strike aircraft, and fast photo-reconnaissance aircraft. It was also used by the British Overseas Airways Corporation (BOAC) as a transport. Source: http://en.wikipedia.org/wiki/De_Havilland_Mosquito, accessed April 28, 2013

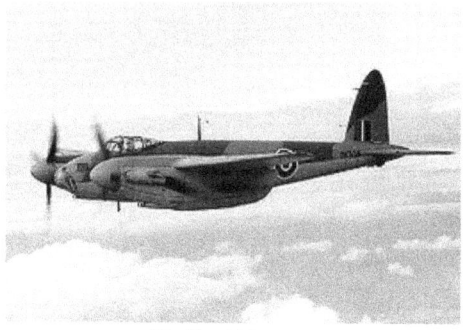

Havilland Mosquito

It was a very active station, all 24 hours of the day. When I went back there several things happened at once that changed my mind about going for the commission. I was working in the Ops Room for only a few weeks when Michael and the Hampshire Regiment was brought back to the mainland but were due to ship out in the near future. He would come and see me quite often. We got very close indeed. When I got some leave he came to see me there, and we became engaged. I was 19 and he just 20. In wartime everything is accelerated. We would have liked to be married, but he thought doing so would be precipitous. The fact that Michael was being sent overseas made things more urgent, so we became unofficially engaged because we hadn't told our parents. We were hoping to meet each other's families so we could get married before his regiment was shipped off. He was to get some leave so we could meet the parents, and we had arranged everything. Then his leave was suddenly cancelled because his regiment was scheduled to leave in two days for North Africa.

I went home for a day or two. Michael wasn't supposed to leave the camp, which was about 20 miles from Surbiton, but he just took off and came to our house there. When it was time for him to return to camp, he and I went to the station hotel, had a glass of sherry and talked until the last train came. He said, "If I should stop a bullet, will you get in touch with my parents?" I thought, *Nothing is going to happen to you, Michael*, and sort of tossed that aside. I went down with him by train to the station near his camp. We said goodbye tearfully, and I took the train back to Surbiton.

He sent me some Chanel No. 5 perfume from Casablanca which he had carefully wrapped it and sealed it with wax. I sat on my bed in the room where I was billeted carefully chipping off the wax with a nail file. The top wouldn't come off, so I gave it a sudden twist and spilt most of it on my RAF-issued bed blanket. I was just heartbroken because you couldn't get decent perfume in Britain then, and I had never had perfume before. Anytime anyone came into my room they said, "Oh, what a heavenly perfume! What is it?" When I left Tangmere I asked permission to buy the blanket, but they said, "No. Just take it with you." So I did have Michael's perfume with me, but not on me. Soon after, his letters stopped coming.

Then I learned they thought my mother was terminally ill with pleurisy. I was given compassionate leave to go back and be with her. The doctors didn't think she would last the night, but, of course, a few weeks later she was up doing her usual things as if nothing had happened. It was just another of those things that confounded the medical profession because my mother lived to be nearly 107 years old, outliving all of these doctors of doom.

About the same time I heard that my favorite cousin, Terrence Minns, had been blown up over the North Sea. Oh, I mourned his loss. But one didn't have time in the war to really mourn one's loved ones. You just had to carry on; everything became so hectic. I found these things emotionally very taxing for me.

I developed hives which I had never heard of before, but I got these big knots which came out on the back of my hand, traveled up my forearms and up to my head. I was taken to an RAF recovery home. A civilian doctor we used to refer to me as his spotted lady. This was in the winter. I felt the cold terribly, but I was still burning up. I would lie on top of the bed with just a sheet over me and you could see the steam rising from my arms and my body. I was just burning up with these wretched hives, and they didn't go away until they went all the way down my body to my feet. To this day, I still don't know why. The doctor said, "It could be stress, or it could be this or that or the other," so I really never knew what that was, but it took a toll on me.

A week or two before I was supposed to go to take the code and cipher course, I was in the Ops Room on duty. I had gone on break when another girl came out and said, "Have you seen the *Daily Telegraph* today?" I said, "No." She said, "I think you should take a look." And there was Michael's name listed as killed in action fighting Rommel's army in North Africa. It was a terrible shock to find out about it that way. But, of course, I had to go back on duty.

That's war.

This to me was incomprehensible! I just couldn't bear it. I was really devastated by Michael's death. I just couldn't face going to Ops. I suppose in a way it would have been the thing to get my mind preoccupied, but I somehow just sort of collapsed. I just couldn't think about that.

The first leave I had, I wrote Michael's parents a letter, expressed my sympathy and explained who I was and said I would like to meet them. This was a wish of Michael's, and I would certainly like to honor that if they felt up to seeing me. Joan Cuddon, the mother, immediately wrote back and said, "Of course, we know all about you and we want to see you." They asked me to come visit them.

They had a house down on the west coast. I remember stepping out of this little diesel train (I had never been on a diesel train before). I was walking up the lane towards where they lived, and Joan was walking down this little country lane to the station. She threw her arms around me, and we just started crying. I was so filled with emotion, I didn't know what to say.

Michael's father, who was a brigadier in the Hampshire Regiment, was a tall, handsome man. He was equally welcoming to this girl he didn't know. They are a wonderful family. Their other son, Charles, whose real name was John Anthony, was at a public school near Reading run by Benedictines. But they weren't cloistered, so to speak. It was called Douai, but I think it was affiliated with monastery in France, which they pronounced Dou-way. I think Charles was about sixteen years old at the time. He was also grief stricken with Michael's death. We went to visit him at the school.

Charles said that if the war hadn't ended by the time he was old enough to fight, he would have been a conscientious objector, which would have troubled his father who was a Brigadier General in the Hampshire Regiment. He later published books and plays and wrote for newspapers. So that's how I got to meet the Cuddons, who became friends for a long time. I just regretted that we couldn't have been a full family.

That was a very heart-wrenching position for me. I just had to give up all hope of going to code and cipher training. I couldn't think straight really, and I knew I just couldn't go through that course. About the same time at Tangmere they asked for three volunteers to go to Ford night fighter station, which had been made into a Type 1 station, which meant that it could facilitate any kind of aircraft—American, English or whatever. That meant that the control tower required three watch-keepers. We didn't really know the full significance of it at the time, but I thought, *Oh, well, that will be a change. I will get away. I will go to Ford and actually be working on an airfield*, although not with my beloved Spitfires but with the Mosquito night fighters that would be stationed there. Two other girls and I volunteered for Ford. One of them, Rochelle Wine, lived in Little Hampton, which was one of the nearest towns to Ford. She wanted to be near her parents who had come from Poland just before the war. The other girl was named Joanne.

Chapter Fifteen

FORD NIGHT FIGHTER STATION, CLOSE CALL #1, "THE CIRCUS," GERMAN DEFECTORS

So we three repaired to Ford,[1] which turned out to be quite a shock for us because ever since we had joined the service, we Ops girls had all been treated as potential officer material. We previously had our own house staff and kitchen. Now we were assigned to a house that stood alone right by the runway with absolutely no heating of any kind. The house had been built just before the war and had not been finished up inside. Nobody lived in it, the walls sweated in the winter; my bed was permanently damp. We could only have one hot bath a week, which meant I had to cycle to, to the other end of the station. If the weather was cold, it was just too

---

[1] Ford is a village and civil parish in the Arun District of West Sussex, England. It is located 3 km (two miles) to the south-west of Arundel. The civil parish, roughly triangular in shape, covers an area of 414.69 hectares (1,024.7 acres) and has a population of 1358 according to the 2001 census. The parish is also the location of HM Prison Ford, otherwise known as Ford Open Prison, and situated on the site of the former RAF Ford Battle of Britain airfield and Royal Naval Air Station (*HMS Peregrine*). Source: http://en.wikipedia.org/wiki/RAF_Ford, accessed April 22, 2013

bad. You come out of a hot bath into freezing cold weather and then cycled back home again. That was the only time I experienced hot water just once a week. We went to the housing officer and said, "This is quite impossible. There is no heating of any kind." Of course, the usual thing was flung at us. "Well, don't you know there's a war on," et cetera.

Most of the time I'd been in the service I was used to being surrounded by lots of other WAAF friends. There were 50 or 60 of us in Special Duty at Tangmere. There was always someone to be with, play tennis with, or go out to have fun with. But I had nothing much in common with the two I came to Ford with because they had been on other watches. There was lovely countryside around there, and I enjoyed roaming around on my bicycle. However, I did miss the companionship of many of the girls I knew.

The first shock we had was when we reported to the control tower and to our CO, squadron leader Tommy Thompson. He was a rather austere young Scotsman who was only about 24 but looked about 35. In giving us instructions about what our duties were he ended up by saying, "And I don't want you interfering with the airmen." We looked at each other in astonishment and said, "Exactly what do you mean, sir, by interfering with the airmen?" He said, "You heard me. I know what you WAAFs are like." We said, "How can you possibly know? We have only just arrived here!" He said, "Well, just remember what I said."

We were all about to go back to Tangmere and tell them, "We don't want to go to Ford," but in war time, you can't do that. So we had to bite the bullet, but we were unhappy. We weren't treated at all the way we were used to being treated before. We also worked staggered hours. I attempted several times to go to the mess, which was about half a mile away from where I was. I'd have to go up a long road, and invariably I found that if I came off duty at one o'clock, they had finished serving. If I had to go on duty at five o'clock, they hadn't started serving dinner. I practically spent all my money on just cycling into Little Hampton or Arundel, which was another town nearby, to find something to eat. Otherwise, I would have starved at Ford.

Nearby Arundel Castle was the seat of the Duke of Norfolk, which I never quite understood. If this was the seat of the Duke of Norfolk, what was he doing in Sussex? The duke's cousin was the CO of the station.

The officers, not the other ranks, were always invited there for different things. I did go once escorted by an officer because a very famous pianist was giving a concert at the castle. I went under the glaring eyes of WAAF officers who didn't think it was my place to be there, but I enjoyed that, and also seeing inside the castle.

The Operations Room was not very large; rather crowded, in fact. There was a telephonist at her board and three radio operators sitting in a row communicating with aircraft. At the end of a long table was a TR9 bomber frequency, which I think was on a 12-mile radius. In front of the window was a wing-shaped desk. I sat at one end, the duty pilot sat at the other end, and in the center in front of the console were two controllers. On the wall in front of us were three loudspeakers. One was the local frequency for our airfield [call sign Coach Ride], one was Fighter Command, and then there was the U. S. Air Force Command. The speakers were always crackling with pilots asking permission to taxi out, to land, or whatever. The TR9 frequency also picked up "skip" [programs] like opera from Milan, something from France, and music-while-you-work from the BBC. So there was a constant cacophony of sounds apart from conversations everybody was having with aircrew. We had to keep the doors opened to the balcony, summer and winter, so the sergeant had access at all times to give us updates on what was happening on the airfield. Aircraft were revving up around us, landing and taking off. It was a very, very noisy room at the best of times.

There was not much relief when one went to bed, since my billet was right beside the runway. At night planes were taking off and landing at different times. During the daytime they were practicing flying or other aircraft were coming and going. Life at Ford was very different from life where I had been stationed before. There were no recreational facilities for the WAAF. So when I came off duty, I had nowhere to go but back to my billet, sit on the side of my damp bed and write letters or read a book with the sound of aircraft landing and taking off right outside my window. It's not very conducive to sleep. I didn't get much rest the whole time I was at Ford. I did try sleeping with a pillow over my head, at the risk suffocating myself, but that didn't shut out the noise.

We worked shift hours. For instance, I would go on duty at 1:00 until 5:00 PM, the next morning I would be on duty from 8:00 AM until 1:00 PM and again at 5:00 PM until 8:00 o'clock the next morning. Then I would have 28 hours off until it started all over again. It was quite intensive working there.

1943. Terry in WAFF uniform, Chichester, Sussex.

One particularly foggy night a plane from another station was in trouble and trying to land with us and mistook a gap in the trees opposite our house for the runway and crashed into the other

Terry (3rd from left) with fellow Ops girls.

side of our house. It was horrifying because I could hear the screams of the pilot. The astonishing thing was that there was some tents put up beyond the house where we had a satellite, so to speak, for squadrons arriving to boost up the manpower on the station. One of the wheels of the crashed aircraft rolled at high speed into the tent and killed a sleeping pilot who had flown all through the Battle of Britain without a scratch. All that and there he was killed by a tire crashing into his tent. What a terrible way to go. It was just terrifying. The whole plane was on fire right beside our house; a very upsetting experience.

They had at the end of the airfield what we called "the circus," which was comprised of captured German bombers and fighters, which had been painted bright yellow. When any new sort of instrument or device was put in our planes, they would take off with the captured German bombers or the fighters and maneuver around to see how efficient our new devices were. The planes were painted bright yellow so that trigger-happy anti-aircraft people didn't fire at the German bombers and fighters. One night our planes had come back from a raid and had just come in to land. The guard at the end of the runway telephoned in that there was a Messerschmitt in the final approach. The controller immediately switched off the airfield lights because the Germans had a habit of coming in on the coattails of our returning planes so they wouldn't be able to be picked up on radar. Then they would come in and strafe the airfield.

But, surprisingly, this plane just landed on the runway. They sent out the sergeant in his jeep to bring the German pilot back, and the plane followed the jeep back to the apron in front of us. Then the pilot came up to the control tower. To our astonishment it was not one man, but two men. Having seen the cockpit of a Messerschmitt, I thought how on earth could two people fit in that, much less one? But they came up with little overnight bags full of rage, fury and indignation. One of them said to our controller, "Is it your usual habit to turn off the lights when a plane is coming in to land?" The controller was taken aback. "I'm so sorry, but I didn't know what your motives were." Our sergeant took the two German pilots up to the mess along with our returning pilots. I heard afterwards that they all had breakfast together and were discussing various maneuvers. Such are the idiosyncrasies of wartime RAF. I guess under the skin they were all brothers when it came to flying.

Messerschmitt cockpit.

One night when I was about to go on duty, we had a raid over. Nothing seemed to happen much, but the control tower called and said, "No unauthorized personnel are to come on the airfield for any reason." Well, of course, I was not unauthorized because I was about to go on duty. But instead of going along the main road up past the hangars, which was a long way around to the control tower, I decided to go around the perimeter of the airfield. It was pitch dark and when I got halfway around, I forgot about the guard at the end of the runway, and he said, "Halt, who goes there!" I dropped everything I had and told him I was going on duty at the control tower. He said, "What are you doing out here on the runway?" I said, "Well, it's a shortcut." He said, "Yes, but you don't understand. They have dropped butterfly bombs all over the airfield." I asked what they were and he said, "They are like of tins of food, but on the top there's a twist sort of like a butterfly, and if you touch that twist or it hits anything, it will explode." So the Germans had successfully immobilized the whole airfield because the aircraft couldn't take off or land with these butterfly bombs everywhere.

He said, "I don't know why you haven't been blown up coming this far. What were you thinking?" I said, "Well, how was I to know that there were butterfly bombs dropped?" So he said, "You can't go back, and you can't go on." This was very familiar. *Didn't the same thing happen on the Isle of Wight?* Anyway I said, "I have to go on. How will *you* get back?" He said, "I've got to stay here until people come and remove the butterfly bombs." I told him, "Well, I can't stay here. I will have to go on." So he said, "Go very carefully, and shuffle along so if you touch anything hard, just try and avoid it." Easier said than done when it was pitch dark. I couldn't see a thing. But I shuffled my way very carefully around the rest of the perimeter until I got to the control tower. When I got inside and went upstairs to the Ops Room, the controller said, "What are you doing here?" I said, "You just said unauthorized personnel, and I didn't know they dropped bombs, butterfly bombs, on the airfield." And he said, "Well, we were going to send the jeep around to tell you not to come as the aircraft aren't going to fly; we're not going to do anything tonight. We're just here to warn other planes that might land here not to come to us. You go home again." Believe me, I went home the long way around.

The next morning there were men situated behind sandbags judiciously popping off these butterfly bombs until the airfield was cleared and in motion again. I thought, *What a clever idea of the Germans to so easily immobilize the whole airfield.* I hate to keep taking off my hat to the Germans, but they were very clever people, one had to admit.

There was an Australian squadron at Ford. There was one young man who didn't speak with an Australian accent, said his grandfather had been, or was, the mayor of Melbourne, a very Victorian-type area in Australia. We used to go out on day trips. I showed him around because I was very familiar with this part of Sussex. The trouble with Andy Kellet was that he was a long way from home, and his mother, I think, as he really wanted somebody to mother him.

One night we were on duty when the duty sergeant called to me from the balcony and said, "There's someone out here who wants to speak to you." So I went outside, and there was Andy. He said, "Oh, darling, I'm in terrible trouble. They have discovered that we're backing up our cars to the bowsers [fuel pumps] and siphoning off the petrol for the planes." I said, "You know, you pilots are the blue-eyed darlings. They are just going to slap you on the hands and tell you not do it again." He said, "You think so?" And I said, "Well, let's hope so, Andy, but you better go back now." Oh, dear, poor chap. But, of course, he was still alive to fly another day without any mishap from the ground.

Occasionally at Ford you'd see a [Westlander] Lysander take off. The Lysander is a small plane with the wing on top of the fuselage, made for landing and taking off on small strips of land. It would take someone to Occupied France or go to pick someone up. These were often people directing French Resistance efforts. We weren't allowed to know too much about them. We had to log everything that took off and landed at Ford except the Lysanders. When one returned, it would taxi to the side of the field. A big black car would meet the plane and drive off with the passenger.

Just before D-Day, we had an American MASH unit arrive to handle the wounded. They set up in a tent beside the airfield. We used to take the wounded their mail and cigarettes to help out the Red Cross. A P-47 (Dakota) brought in wounded and British prisoners-of-war. We had a hanger where they were processed.[2]

Things were really stepping up at Ford. One of the things that came with us was the American field unit, equivalent to MASH, which were bringing nurses in. We thought that's interesting, but what was not so interesting is that we WAAF were being turned out of our house. It was going to be made suitable for these American nurses to live in. We said, "Suitable for them to live in, but it was all right for us to live like this?" And they said, "They have the rank of officers, so we have to get these boilers working and the house heated for them." So with great chagrin we were moved to the other side of the runway to a little row of houses which actually were not so cold. Amazingly, I don't know how it had happened, but my bedroom had two electric heaters in the wall. Other WAAF used

---

[2] The Westland Lysander was a British army co-operation and liaison aircraft produced by Westland Aircraft used immediately before and during the Second World War. After becoming obsolete in the army co-operation role, the aircraft's exceptional short-field performance enabled clandestine missions using small, unprepared airstrips behind enemy lines to place or recover agents, particularly in occupied France with the French Resistance help. Like other British army air co-operation aircraft it was given the name of a mythical or legendary leader, in this case the Spartan general Lysander. Source: http://en.wikipedia.org/wiki/Westland_Lysander, accessed April 14, 2013

to knock at my door all the time saying, "Can we come in and get warm." So it was quite a busy room. But we still had no hot water in the houses there. We special duties people were really peeved about that. I felt for every WAAF, not just us, about these nurses. Just because they were considered officers, they had the whole house turned inside out and made livable for them.

When I moved to that new billet on the other side of the runway, there was a red light on top of the house to warn pilots that there was a building there as they came in to land, especially for pilots from other stations, which didn't know the layout. I could never understand why when people asked where I lived, they roared with laughter when I said, "It's the house by the runway with the red light on top of it." I guess I was really unsophisticated; had absolutely no idea why it was so amusing to them. The penny didn't drop, so to speak, until years later when I was an airhostess with BOAC, and we had landed in Malta overnight on our way to Egypt. The crew and I went down to the harbor. There was something the Royal navy was putting on in the harbor. On our way back, I said, "Why don't we take a short cut up this road? It will save us from going all the way around to get to our hotel," They said, "Oh, we can't go up there." I said, "Why not?" Then they said, "It's the red light district." I innocently asked, "What does that mean?" I must have been about twenty-five at the time. They thought nobody could be twenty-five and not know what that meant, but they explained it to me. I was very embarrassed. Then I remembered in retrospect that's why they were laughing about the red light on top of my house at Ford.

Chapter Sixteen

ENCOUNTER WITH CHURCHILL

When we found out where D-Day was going to be, we realized the importance of Ford being so built up; we were directly opposite the D-Day landings. The military were building a Mulberry [man-made] harbor. Where the D-Day landings were, there wasn't a natural harbor, and they were also going to include a landing strip.[1]

We had sectioned off a certain area on our tarmacs, which would be the length of the landing strip to see which planes could land and take off on that short of a runway. Prime Minister Winston Churchill was coming down to inspect things for himself. The day before he arrived, a flying fortress [B-17], which was beaten up, came in. It was quite dramatic because the pilot had been killed. The copilot had shrapnel in his head, gone berserk and had to be knocked out. Either a radio operator or the navigator had to land the plane, and the poor man had never piloted before. Here he

---

[1] A Mulberry harbor was a portable temporary harbor developed by the British in World War II to facilitate rapid offloading of cargo onto the beaches during the Allied invasion of Normandy. Two prefabricated or artificial military harbors were taken in sections across the English Channel from Britain with the invading army and assembled off the coast of Normandy as part of the D-Day invasion of France in 1944. Source: http://en.wikipedia.org/wiki/Mulberry_harbour, accessed April 22, 2013

was having to land a crippled bomber on a strange airfield, but he made a perfect landing. That was a terrific achievement.

The next day, when I came on duty at eight o'clock, the controllers were frantic. One of them said, "Look, the Prime Minister is coming down this morning, and the field is littered with bombers and fighters that have just dropped out of the sky." We had no room for them on the sidelines. They were all over the field. He said, "And Mr. Churchill can't see the runway. We have got to get these planes off!" So I had to take over the situation. I had woken up with a headache; wasn't in a very good mood, especially as I knew that, except for four hours in the afternoon, I was going to be on duty for the next twenty-four hours. I started calling stations, seeing if the aircraft, whichever were fit, were able to go back to their stations; whether they were open or closed in with weather. Conversely, they were phoning us to find out what had happened to their aircraft, so it was a busy morning,

Churchill's entourage came ahead of him and sort of wafted around our small Ops Room until they got bored. Then one of them sat on the corner of my desk and asked me what I was doing. Here I am very busy, trying to do things, but I tried to be as polite as possible. I got rather irritated with these people coming up, asking me questions, tapping me on the shoulder and saying, "What's that switch for?" And I'd say, "That's the switch that makes announcements to the whole station. Please don't touch it." As I was trying to carry on with these milling people, I forgot about Mr. Churchill coming since he was so late.

The cacophony of sound got very high. I was trying to reach a bomber station somewhere in Cambridge or wherever. As we went through the different exchanges, the voices got fainter and fainter, so I ducked my head under the desk to try to cut out all the noise around me—so I could hear this faint little voice. Suddenly, I got a terrific jab in my back, which made me hit my head on the underside of the desk, which didn't help my headache! This voice boomed, "What are you doing?"

This was the last straw! I just whipped 'round, shook the telephone and said, "What does it look as if I'm doing?" Then I realized I was looking at the grinning face of Mr. Churchill complete with scar. There was dead silence in the room at my terrible blunder. I stood up and said, "Sir, I'm so sorry." He patted me on the shoulder and said, "I'm sorry, my dear, I didn't mean to disturb you."

Then they took him up to the crow's nest, or widow's walk, on top of the station so that he could actually see the runway. I have a photo from a newspaper of him interviewing a young man who landed the flying fortress the day before. Of course, the papers usually got things wrong. They said Ford was an advance U. S. Air Force base.

Prime Minister Winston Churchill

When Mr. Churchill came down to the Ops Room again, I was apprehensive of what my fate would be. Will I be stripped of my rank? Will I be shot at dawn or what? What's the horrible price one has to pay for shouting at one's beloved leader? But he walked to the door, and as tradition, he saluted the desk. Then he winked at me and went out. I remember the nearest controller patted my head and said, "Ms. Terry-Smith, what do you think you were doing?" I said, "Well, it would be nice if one of you had notified me that Mr. Churchill was in the room instead of standing there, preening and letting me to my own devices." They had not much of an answer to that, but it got all around the station. I was very embarrassed because I couldn't explain the circumstances; there didn't seem any way that one could. I think that's the first and last time I ever shouted at anybody. I was absolutely mortified.

A day or two later we had a Mayday from a Lancaster bomber. They were the biggest British bombers. When Prince William and Kate were married [2011], a Lancaster bomber was in the fly-over. I didn't know they were still flying after 70 years, or that one *could* fly after 70 years. Anyway, we had a Mayday. The plane was shot up and they wanted to land. So they came in. When the pilot actually landed, he said, "My brakes are gone." He had lost his starboard, one of his starboard engines, so he had no choice but to pull around to the left and get on the grass area to slow down his speed. Unfortunately, it brought him straight in line with us. So I was on the phone to the pilot's base, who had called me a little earlier to ask for any information about him. I said, "He just landed." The girl on the other end of the phone proceeded to ask me were there any injuries and blah, blah, blah, and I said, "I may have to call you back." She said, "Why?" I said, "Because he's heading straight for our control tower with no brakes!"

The telephone went off. The signal girls and the telephonists had the sense to run to the back of the room, but the controllers just sat there. I thought, *If they are not going to run back, I certainly am not going to. I'll be at my post.* Actually, we were mesmerized. It was like watching a movie. We couldn't believe this huge plane was barreling down straight for us. Miraculously, it stopped on the edge of the apron. I would say it was maybe ten feet from our control tower. Because they didn't have any front wheels in those days, the Lancaster was on a level with our second floor. I remember the pilot up front gazed at us sort of as if he couldn't believe they hadn't crashed into us, and we gazed right back at them. *We* couldn't believe they hadn't crashed into us. After a few moments the controller turned to me and said, "Why didn't you go to the back of the room?" I said, "I wasn't going to the back of the room if you didn't go back." And he said, "Well, we wouldn't go to the back of the room if you didn't go back." I thought, *Good heavens, we were playing chicken. It's a crazy war.*

Chapter Seventeen

LEONARD CHESHIRE, D-DAY, WRONG-WAY GLIDER, WOMAN PILOT, INTERROGATION

There were two things that occurred before D-Day that impressed me very much. One night a Mosquito, not one of ours, landed at our field. The pilot came up into the control tower. His name was Leonard Cheshire, a wing commander and pathfinder for his bomber command. That meant he flew under the bombers, targeting places they were to bomb with more accuracy. I gather that he had been doing this in Germany, France and Italy. That evening he stopped at Ford to refuel. He came and sat beside me, a very tall dark young man with beetling [heavy] eyebrows—that's what I remember about him—and very long fingers. He sat there beside me quite polite, but obviously not encouraging conversation, which I understood. I imagined he was rather introspective and probably wanted to concentrate on what he had to do ahead of him, but he took out some chewing gum and offered me one. I knew it was out of politeness, so I said, "No, thank you." He said, "Go on take it." So I took it from him, but I felt dirty afterwards thinking, *I know chewing gum is the only way they can relieve the tension, and maybe I've taken one away from him that he really needed.* I really over-think these things.

It transpired that he was a very remarkable person who had been awarded the Victoria Cross and the DSO (Distinguished Service Order). He was an amazing person. Of course, I knew nothing about bomber commands, so knew nothing about his career, but afterwards I discovered an awful lot about him. I was most impressed with the fact that he had been made the youngest group captain at the age of twenty-five, the youngest group captain in the RAF, but had wanted to belong to this squadron of dambusters and had left a desk job that they put him in. I think he did 102 missions. That's amazing to think that he could do that, or anyone could do that. But anyway, he joined 617 Squadron with a demoted rank of wing commander.

When the bombs were dropped on Nagasaki, Cheshire was one of the official observers. He was amazed at how much damage that bomb could do compared with the damage that took so many of the squadrons of bombers to do in Europe. After the war he had a breakdown, not surprising, and went to rehabilitation. When he came out, people appeared at his doorstep who were dying or very ill. He started an amazing foundation, Leonard Cheshire Disability Charity for people who were sick, homeless and afflicted regardless of their color or race. This grew to I think about 248 homes in 51 countries—amazing achievements. He also became a Roman Catholic and changed his life completely. He was a most extraordinary person. Even him just sitting beside me, I felt this is somebody different from the usual pilots that used to come into the control tower. I was very proud that I had spent a few moments in his presence. That's how I honestly remember him—powerful in his own way.[1]

---

1 Group Captain Geoffrey Leonard Cheshire, Baron Cheshire, VC, OM, DSO and Two Bars,

The most memorable thing that has stayed in my mind on D-Day was in the early evening just before dusk the sky seemed to be absolutely filled, with planes. I guess they were [Douglas] C-47s. I can't remember what the planes were, but they were towing gliders en masse. The sky was just filled with them as they flew over and passed us, it was a spectacular sight. We knew D-Day was on.

Later that night, the duty pilot called out that something had landed at the other end of the airfield. We had nothing on radar, no Maydays, and no one had called us. We were bewildered as to what it was, so we sent our company sergeant, Harry Greenbaum, out in the jeep to find out what was going on. When he got to the end of the airfield, he found a glider that had landed back on our airfield. It had crash-landed and was at an angle. The men were struggling to get out of the plane. Their faces were blackened, and apparently Harry said to them, "Oy! Where the hell do you think you are?"

And one turned to the other and said, "Blimey, he speaks good English for a Jerry, doesn't he!" Harry had to point out to them that they hadn't landed in France. They landed back in England. The men burst into tears. Apparently, on the way over, when the pilot ahead of them released the towing rope, they turned on a reciprocal bearing. They didn't realize they weren't still heading for France and landed back in England after all that training.

But perhaps they were the lucky ones, because we heard some of the glider teams crashed on landing and had been killed or were being immediately captured by the Germans.

DFC (7 September 1917–31 July 1992) was a highly decorated British RAF pilot during the Second World War. Among the honors Cheshire received as a pilot, is the Victoria Cross, the highest and most prestigious award for gallantry in the face of the enemy that can be awarded to British and Commonwealth forces. He was the youngest Group Captain in the RAF and one of the most highly decorated pilots of the War but after serving as the British observer on the Nagasaki nuclear attack he resigned from the Air Force. He founded a hospice which grew into the charity Leonard Cheshire Disability and he became known for his work in conflict resolution; he was created Baron Cheshire in 1991 in recognition of his charitable work. Source: http://en.wikipedia.org/wiki/Leonard_Cheshire, accessed April 23, 2013

1944, Ford. Terry Smith (right).

In the months following, we had over a thousand Dakotas transporting prisoners of war and the wounded back to our base, which kept the MASH people pretty busy. They set up a sort of temporary hospital there. When we were off duty we would go talk to these soldiers, mail letters for them back to America or wherever in England, and bring them cigarettes, et cetera. They nicknamed us Angels of Mercy, which was rather amusing.[2]

But things were really busy all the time with planes returning, just being able to sort of totter back to the coast and crash land with us. On one occasion, in less than an hour all three runways had been closed because of planes crashing one after the other. Our planes that were leaving had to take off on the grass and miss the crashed planes on the runways. Our lost planes were frequently replaced by

---

2 The Douglas C-47 Skytrain or Dakota (RAF designation) is a military transport aircraft that was developed from the Douglas DC-3 airliner. It was used extensively by the Allies during World War II and remained in front line service with various military operators through the 1950s. . . . In Europe, the C-47 and a specialized paratroop variant, the C-53 Skytrooper, were used in vast numbers in the later stages of the war, particularly to tow gliders and drop paratroops. In the Pacific, with careful use of the island landing strips of the Pacific Ocean, C-47s were even used for ferrying soldiers serving in the Pacific theater back to the United States. C-47s (approx. 2,000 received under lend-lease) in British and Commonwealth service took the name Dakota, from the acronym "DACoTA" for *Douglas Aircraft Company Transport Aircraft*. The C-47 also earned the informal nickname *Gooney Bird* in the European theater of operations. Source: http://en.wikipedia.org/wiki/Douglas_C-47_Skytrain, accessed April 22, 2013

the ATA, Air Transport Auxiliary organization, which were civilian fliers who would fly the new aircraft from the factories direct to whichever airfield required them. Planes leaving the factories had no RT [Radio Transmission] because the factory personnel didn't know the frequency of the stations the planes would ultimately be assigned to. We didn't know what frequency the factory planes were on, and we didn't use a universal transmission frequency, so we had no way of contacting them. The planes would also leave the factory painted in camouflage with RAF insignia, then would be repainted with the station's insignias when they got to us.

Once, when one of them was being delivered to us, the plane kept flying around and around making no attempt to land. We fired a Very pistol [flare gun] with green smoke, indicating that it was okay to land. Sometimes when planes would come in with no radio, we would fire a red flare indicating that it was not okay to land the plane, or a green flare, depending on the situation. Well, this plane still wouldn't land. We thought maybe his air speed indicator [ASI] had malfunctioned. So they sent up a Mosquito to get in front of this plane to lead it in at the right speed, but the other plane sheared away from the Mosquito and still went on going around the circuit. Finally it came in to land and pulled up in front of our apron. A small woman got out of the plane, came up storming up to the control tower and said, "What fool sent that plane around in front of me?" She said, "My wheels would not come down. They were jammed. I had to get down on one knee and pump away manually to get it down, meanwhile steering with the other hand. But this darn plane kept getting in front of me, and I nearly crashed into it." The controller tried to explain that we thought her ASI wasn't working. She was a bit mollified after that. But that was one of the tricky things about the planes being delivered unmarked without knowing what squadron they were going to and without any RT.

Ford Night Fighter Station Operations Staff. Terry Smith front row, middle.

One day when I was about to go off duty, I was told that as the only senior NCO on the field I had to go to this particular hangar where they were holding a woman who had come in one of the Dakotas. She didn't have the right papers, and she only spoke German, or they thought it was German. I would have to interrogate her and strip her to see if she had any hidden code messages or something. I don't know what *they* were looking for, and I certainly didn't know what *I* was supposed to be looking for. So I went along to this poor woman looking utterly bewildered who didn't know why she was standing in this hangar. I took her to a small room inside the hangar and with great difficulty mimed that she had to take off her clothes. It was quite cold. I felt very sorry for her as I was wearing a great coat myself, so I took it off and put it on her while I examined her clothes. I don't know what I was looking for. I just felt the pockets, the linings and around the hems to see if there were any hidden messages and found nothing. I reported that she seemed a perfectly innocent civilian and to please have someone take care of her, which I hope they did. It was embarrassing for both of us.

Chapter Eighteen

"WE YANKS," HAROLD CARVER, BUTTERED POPCORN, MOSQUITO RIDE

The annual leave that I got from this circus that was going on twenty-four, day and night, was to shoot out to London to see my family in their second apartment and fourth home since the war began. I had the luxury of being in a warm place, in a warm bed, having a warm bath, which was shear luxury. It made me appreciate my home twice as much with all the years I had been deprived of it.

We had an American controller come to us for a while who was very bombastic and did rather put our backs up because about the first thing he said was, "We Yanks have come over here to finish the job that you Brits don't seem to be able to do—getting rid of the Germans." I don't think there was one person at that control tower who hadn't had somebody die or missing, and our own NCO, Tommy Thompson, had been shot down during the Battle of Britain. We had a 10 or 20-mile radius around London called the IAZ, Inter-Artillery Zone, where our fighters chasing

German planes were supposed to break off and let the attack guns take over. We also had barrage balloons to deter the bombers from diving down low to bomb London. Apparently Tommy Thompson got so enthusiastic on the tail of this German plane that he didn't realize he had gone into the IAZ, and he was shot down by our own guns and lost half of his stomach and seemed to exist mainly on milk. He was just so thin—a rail. No wonder he had such a sour disposition. One can imagine that he suffered quite a bit. And to hear this American saying, "Well, you know, you've made a mess of this, so we're coming to straighten you out," didn't go down well with us as everyone in that room had lost a loved one. Tommy Thompson didn't say anything. He just looked down at the floor. That particular American wasn't very popular, and we were glad to see him go. But you can't judge everybody by one person.

One day I was very busy on the telephone, and there was an unusual terrible noise going on. A Thunderbolt had landed after being damaged in some way and taxied right up to our apron, and the pilot was trying to get the engine going again. It made a terrific sound, and I was having difficulty hearing the person on the other end of the phone. The pilot came up to the control tower to report. He was a very slim, nice-looking young fairhaired American named Harold Carver. After speaking to the controller and waiting for transport to take him up to the offices, he came over and spoke to me and apologized and said, "I'm sure I made an awful noise with my revving my plane," and I said, "Yes, you did." I sort of apologized and said, "Well, I know you had to do what you had to do, and it was difficult to hear for a while." But he was so unusual.

I can't remember after all this time how our friendship evolved, but he would write to me, and I'd write back to him because I didn't know where he was, just an APO address. Then I was going on some leave and he was going on leave, and I said, "Why don't you come and stay with my family?" as he had nowhere particular to go. So he came and stayed with me and my parents and my sister. They all enjoyed him so much.

Harold Carver and Terry

My father was allowed to have a car as a surveyor. He showed Harold different parts of the area we lived in. One night he asked us if we had ever had popcorn before, and no, we hadn't, so he asked for a Dutch oven and poured in some oil and the popcorn. We were fascinated. He said, "Popcorn isn't worth anything unless you have butter on it." He used big slab of butter, which was about a ration for our family for a month. We sort of watched in agony as he poured this melted butter all over the popcorn. Of course, we couldn't say anything, and we wouldn't have done so anyway. So no doubt about it, we sucked every bit of butter off each piece of popcorn. We had a delightful time.

While he was away from his squadron, they had converted from Thunderbolts to Mustangs. When he returned, he had just time to familiarize himself with the cockpit when he had to go up on a sortie. He was shot down and was a prisoner of war until the end of the war.

Another incident was comical in retrospect, but not really funny at the time. The CO of the control tower, Tommy Thompson, got in his head that it would be a good idea if we experienced in some small way what the pilots go through. So he asked for volunteers to go up and find out. Well, of course, I immediately sprang up and said, "Me, me, me, please, sir," because my ambition all my life was to fly and never had the opportunity. I could just see myself up in a Mosquito—what a thrill! Of course, it didn't turn out that way. Actually, the others really didn't want to go up and experience what the pilots did, so I was the only one to volunteer. They said, "Oh, no, you're going up in the reconnaissance plane." I said, "Well, that's better than nothing." They told me to wear trousers, which I didn't normally wear except at night and as my uniform. It was quite a cold day, but I didn't know what it was going to be like in the air. They put this parachute on me, which was very uncomfortable, heavy, and I sort of waddled along to the aircraft. The pilot and navigator were going to be very warm because they were wearing fur-lined flying boots and fur-lined jackets, but I was just there in my little uniform.

I got in and we taxied out and got in line with the Mosquitoes who were going on the night-flying test. We, the recce [reconnaissance] were going to do a night-flying test, too. We were in line with this terrific noise from all the other twin-engine bombers roaring away.

One of the things I did not appreciate was the absolutely horrible racket that went on the whole time. The inside of the plane was so noisy, the pilot and the navigator had to yell back at me. My voice was rather soft, so they couldn't hear me. I would have to stagger up to the seats, yell back at them and then go sit down again. We were just given permission to taxi onto the runway when I looked back and saw that the door to the aircraft had swung open. I yelled up to them, but they couldn't hear me. I yelled again and said, "Stop! We can't go yet the doors have come open!" They looked at me and said, "Well, go shut it." So okay, I staggered back down the aircraft again, leaned against the doorjamb and reached around with my hand, but the door had gone flush with the plane. I tried to reach it, but my arm wasn't long enough, and the parachute was pushing me out of the plane. I managed to jerk myself back in again and tried leaning against the left door jamb sideways, reaching out with one hand, holding on to something on the inside of the aircraft with other, but still I couldn't reach it.

I was about to fall out of the aircraft with the weight of this parachute pushing me out, and the pilot and navigator in the Mosquito behind me were roaring with laughter. They thought it was so funny. I wasn't a bit amused because, for one thing, the propellers were churning out lots of dust and whatever else was lying around on the tarmac, and I could hardly see for all this dust flying around in my face. I tried to yell back to the cockpit crew and tell them I couldn't shut the door. One of them looked back and saw that I was in a predicament, so he came back and, being taller, of course, although I was five-foot-seven, he was about six foot, said, "You hold on to me while I lean out and close the door," so we did that managing to slam it shut. We went back and I sat down in my seat. But the whole time we were flying, I kept looking out of the corner of my eye, watching this door. I thought, *If that comes open mid-air, I will be sucked out of there.* I do have a parachute; however, it depends how high we are.

The pilot said, "We're not going up very high." I don't know what they were doing with their instruments. But anyway, I think we only went up maybe 3,000, 5,000 feet. I thought, *Well, if I have to—if I'm sucked out, I might be too low to the ground to do anything. What an ignominious way to die.* Then, *Supposing I had fallen out of the aircraft while I was trying to shut the door. You know, that would have been ending my life with a whimper rather than a bang.* But we flew around for a while. The plane had a bomb bay. I guess they could drop bombs as well. I can't remember what make of plane it was now, but they said, "If you can lie down there, you can see we're going over the English Channel. You might see something interesting." So with great difficulty, with this parachute on, I laid down. It was quite astonishing to see the sea rushing under me. I did see some quite interesting things, too. When I landed back on the ground, it took me some time to get my sea legs again. I was freezing to death because it was very cold in there, but I guess in a way the parachute had kept me warm. When I got back to the control tower, everybody said, "Well, how was it? Did you enjoy it?" I said, "Yes, it was wonderful." I have flown under better conditions since then, that is for sure.

By then, my sister, Sylvia, had left the BBC overseas service and had gone to work in the Foreign Office's Intelligence Bureau. I don't know how that happened, but she was in Italy attached to General Mark Clark's U. S. Army outfit, having the rank of captain. She was in charge of the psychological warfare bureau there where she had people working under her getting out fliers to drop over German lines. She edited a newspaper for the forces. I guess it was the *Stars and Stripes* in that area. She also broadcast to them; had quite a hectic time there. At the time, I knew nothing of this. I had no idea where she was except if we wanted to write to her, we had to send it to an APO address. It was all very mysterious.[1]

---

1 Mark Wayne Clark (May 1, 1896–April 17, 1984) was an American general during World War II and the Korean War and was the youngest lieutenant general (three-star general) in the U.S. Army. During World War I, he commanded a company of soldiers in 1917 and was seriously wounded by shrapnel. After the war, Clark's abilities were noticed by General George Marshall. During World War II, he was the USA's Commander in Italy. He is known for his triumphal entry into Rome in 1944, the first major Axis city to fall. Some detractors say he ignored the orders of his British superior officer, and they blame him for the escape of the German 10th Army which he let slip in his pursuit for the glory of entering Rome first. The German 10th Army joined with their countrymen at the Transimene Line. Clark became the youngest American to be promoted to general in 1945. General Dwight D. Eisenhower considered him a brilliant staff officer and trainer. Clark won many awards, including the Distinguished Service Cross for extreme bravery in war, subordinate only to the Medal of Honor. . . . From 1954 until 1965, after retiring from the Army, General Clark served as president of The Citadel, the prestigious military college located in Charleston, South Carolina . . . He wrote two memoirs:

HER FINEST HOUR

She was at some big reception given for the Italian guerillas who were defending that part of the country. There was a big ball given for them. They came in their outfits with these bands across their bodies with all these bullets in them. Apparently it was a very crowded dance floor as Sylvia was dancing with one of these men and, in the crush, he managed to break some of her ribs, which wasn't a very good experience for her. Another time when she was in London, she was coming from the underground on the escalator, where she encountered some GIs in front of her with their kit bags. When she got to the top of the escalator onto the platform, the GI in front of her slung his kit bag over his shoulder, knocked her down and broke her wrist. So that was one occasion.

The other one was the civilian happening. I went to visit her one time when she was with the BBC, at the sea service, when they were evacuated to Evesham in Worcestershire. She rented a horse from a nearby stable to practice her jumping. The man informed her he just had one horse left, and she says, "That's fine. Is he a jumper?" He said, "Oh, yes, he is." She trotted out, and when she got up to this first fence, the horse suddenly stopped right at the fence and tossed her over, then jumped over on top of her and fractured her pelvis. While she was lying on the field, the owner of the riding stables had the nerve to come up and ask her for her fee. She discovered afterwards that this horse was actually blind in one eye, which he hadn't informed her about, so that when she took him up to the fence, it was on his blind side. He didn't see the fence until got right up to it.

Calculated Risk (1950) and *From the Danube to the Yalu* (1954). . . . An interstate spur (I-526) in the suburbs of Charleston, South Carolina, was named Mark Clark Expressway in his honor. Source: http://en.wikipedia.org/wiki/Mark_W._Clark, accessed June 29, 2013

Chapter Nineteen

THE BLITZ, BUZZ BOMBS, CLOSE CALL #2, SIR MICHAEL BRUCE, "GRAVEDIGGER DICK"

During the Blitz, the first buzz bomb [V-1 flying bomb] that we saw came right over our airfield at Ford with a report that there was a plane on fire. We went to look at it. There were no reports of Mayday or anything, so we all stood on the balcony and watched it whiz by as it crashed in the next field. When a buzz bomb stopped, that meant the gyro had shut off, and the bomb was about to come down. When you didn't hear anything, that's when you dove for cover.

V-1 "Buzz" Bomb

HER FINEST HOUR

I had to admire the Germans. I thought, *My gosh, they were really on target if they were aiming at Ford.* It was just that that gyro was just a little bit off. The RAF regiment started firing at it, but fortunately they were rotten shots. Otherwise, I wouldn't be telling you about this.[1,2]

---

1 The Blitz (from German, "lightning") was the sustained strategic bombing of the United Kingdom by Germany during the Second World War. Between 7 September 1940 and 21 May 1941 there were major raids (attacks in which more than 100 tons of high explosives were dropped) on 16 British cities. Over a period of 267 days (almost 37 weeks), London was attacked 71 times, Birmingham, Liverpool and Plymouth eight times, Bristol six, Glasgow five, Southampton four, Portsmouth three, and there was also at least one large raid on another eight cities. This was a result of a rapid escalation starting on 24 August 1940, when night bombers aiming for RAF airfields drifted off course and accidentally destroyed several London homes, killing civilians, combined with Churchill's immediate response of bombing Berlin. Starting on 7 September 1940, London was bombed by the Luftwaffe for 57 consecutive nights. More than one million London houses were destroyed or damaged, and more than 40,000 civilians were killed, almost half of them in London. Ports and industrial centers outside London were also heavily attacked; the major Atlantic sea port of Liverpool was the most heavily bombed city outside London, suffering nearly 4,000 dead. Other ports including Bristol, Cardiff, Hull, Portsmouth, Plymouth, Southampton, and Swansea were also targeted, as were the industrial cities of Birmingham, Belfast, Coventry, Glasgow and Manchester. Birmingham and Coventry were heavily targeted because of the Spitfire and tank factories in Birmingham and the many munitions factories in Coventry; the city center of Coventry was almost completely destroyed. Source: http://en.wikipedia.org/wiki/The_Blitz, accessed June 2, 2013

2 The V-2 (German: *Vergeltungswaffe 2*, "retaliation weapon 2"), technical name Aggregat-4 (A4), was a short-range ballistic missile that was developed during the Second World War in Germany, specifically targeted at London and later Antwerp. Commonly referred to as the V-2 rocket, the liquid-propellant rocket was the world's first long-range combat-ballistic missile and first known human artifact to enter outer space. It was the progenitor of all modern rockets, including those used by the United States and Soviet Union's space programs. During the aftermath of World War II the American, Soviet and British governments all gained access to the V-2's technical designs as well as the actual German scientists responsible for creating the rockets, via Operation Paperclip, Operation Osoaviakhim and Operation Backfire respectively. The weapon was presented by Nazi propaganda as a retaliation for the bombers that attacked ever more German cities from 1942 until Germany surrendered. Beginning in September 1944, over 3,000 V-2s were launched as military rockets by the German Wehrmacht against Allied targets during the war, mostly London and later Antwerp and Liège. According to a BBC documentary in 2011, the attacks resulted in the deaths of an estimated 9,000 civilians and military personnel, while 12,000 forced laborers and concentration camp prisoners were killed producing the weapons. Source: https://en.wikipedia.org/wiki/V-2_rocket, June 2, 2013

German V-2 Rocket

Another time I was going home for a spot of leave. The train would go up to Victoria, so I would change at Clapham Junction to get on the Waterloo Line. No one hung about in those days. You got out and rushed to wherever you were going. As it was a cold day I thought, *I have 20 minutes. I'll go over to the waiting room.* I was just about to open the door when a man rushed past me, took the handle out of my hand and slammed the door in my face. I stood there saying to myself, "Really, how terribly rude." All of a sudden there was the most almighty bang, and the whole station shook. Lights fell off and signs fell down. I hadn't heard the buzz bomb because as I got off the train, the gyro cut off. That's why I didn't hear it coming down. When I'd go to London on leave to my parents' flat, I'd hear buzz bombs overhead. They sounded like motorbikes. One would like in bed thinking, *Is that a buzz bomb or a motorcycle?*

Buzz bombs weren't much fun. We did have a deterrent by then. Later in the war, 1944, we had [Gloster] Meteor jet fighter aircraft. They could only fly for 20 minutes before they had to land; run out of fuel. The first one I saw was coming from a nearby base to us, but he was so low on fuel that he couldn't circle to land with us. So, he just sort of went on past us getting lower and lower until he came down in a cabbage field half a mile away. These jets could keep up with the buzz bombs. They would get under the wing of the buzz bomb and tip it, so that it fell into fields instead of the cities and towns they were aiming for. Of course, there was one we could do nothing about. Later on, when Germany had the V-2 rockets, theses rockets would go up in the air and just come down anywhere. We were very vulnerable against them.[3]

Gloster Meteor

When I was first issued my uniforms, I was always given black shoes that were most uncomfortable; they would rub my skin raw. I would get blisters and then they would burst. Oh, my feet were a mess. I had a permit from the RAF medical officer where I was stationed that allowed me to wear civilian shoes. Miraculously, when I did go to buy them, I found a pair of very comfortable shoes with a rounded toe and crepe soles in exactly the same colors as my uniform. What were the chances of finding a pair of shoes that

---

3 The Gloster Meteor was the first British jet fighter and the Allies' first operational jet aircraft. The Meteor's development was heavily reliant on its ground-breaking turbojet engines, developed by Sir Frank Whittle and his company, Power Jets Ltd. Development of the aircraft began in 1940, work on the engines had started in 1936. The Meteor first flew in 1943 and commenced operations on 27 July 1944 with 616 Squadron of the Royal Air Force (RAF). Although the Meteor was not an aerodynamically advanced aircraft, it proved to be a successful and effective combat fighter. Source: http://en.wikipedia.org/wiki/Gloster_Meteor, accessed June 2, 2013

color? They were so comfortable and made all the world difference in walking comfort. But I was continuously being stopped by MPs and had to drag out my chit to show I had permission to wear these shoes.

One thing I disliked very much was going to dances in that uniform; wearing these soled shoes. It was almost impossible to dance! You couldn't slide your feet across the ground. So one day another WAAF persuaded me to go to a dance. She didn't want to go to the officers' mess and dance by herself, so I went with her. I told her, "I'm not going to dance, but I will go with you." When we got up there, I hung in the background, bought myself a drink and just sort of tried to fade into the wallpaper. Unfortunately, I was accosted by this (I thought) elderly person. He was probably about twenty-five, but he seemed quite old to me. He was in charge of the RAF regiment that was supposed to go out to a surrounding airfield. He asked me to dance. I said, "No, thank you. I really can't dance because I have these crepe-soled shoes." He said, "Oh, that shouldn't deter a young lady like you. We'll just hop around."

So very reluctantly I did dance with him and was having to lift up my feet all the time. Otherwise, I would be sticking to the ground. He had the most uncomfortable way of dancing, sort of bobbing from side to side; almost made me seasick. I saw some of my friends looking vastly amused at my predicament. He told me that his name as Michael Bruce. Apparently, he was Sir Michael Bruce, and he sort of took a shine to me. Unfortunately, he wouldn't leave me alone. I said, "I really feel very uncomfortable dancing in these shoes, so please go; don't think of staying with me. I'm sure there are other young ladies you would prefer to dance with." He said, "No, no! I want to sit and talk to you." He told me about himself. He said, "I have a brother, Nigel Bruce, who is a film star." I said, "Oh, yes, I've seen him in films." "Oh yes," he said, "he's a blot on the family escutcheon." We've never had an actor in our family before. But I couldn't help thinking, *I bet up in Scotland in our drafty castle, you probably rather envy Nigel making enough money to be living in very comfortable circumstances in Hollywood.*

I remember once seeing Nigel Bruce as Dr. Watson in one of those Sherlock Holmes films shot during the war or just before the war. He always portrayed stuffy generals or colonels. We were talking about things that we liked, and I said I loved the theater. He said, "Oh, well, how about going out to London one evening to the theater? No funny business." But I somehow managed to wriggle out of that situation. He was a perfectly nice person, but I thought he was terribly old. Anyway, that was Sir Michael Bruce. I got teased by the control tower personnel the next day. When I went on duty they opened the door with a flourish and said, "Enter, Lady Bruce!" They teased me for several days.[45]

---

4 Sir Michael William Selby Bruce, 11th Baronet (27 March 1894–20 May 1957) was an author and adventurer. The son of Sir William Waller Bruce, 10th Baronet, of West Drayton, Middlesex, director of an art gallery, Michael Bruce entered Abingdon School, then joined the British South Africa Police as a trooper (1913). After First World War service with the Royal Artillery at Gallipoli and on the Western Front, Bruce became a traveler, largely in Africa and South America, and an author and newspaper columnist. During the Second World War he served in a barrage balloon unit, with 901 (County of London) squadron, Royal Air Force Regiment. Later in the war he was Senior Weapons Instructor for glider pilots at Bridgnorth. He was the elder brother of Nigel Bruce, the actor. Michael Bruce died at Vancouver, British Columbia. Source: http://en.wikipedia.org/wiki/Sir_Michael_Bruce,_11th_Baronet, accessed June 15, 2013

5 William Nigel Ernle Bruce (4 February 1895–8 October 1953) . . . known as Nigel Bruce, was a British character actor on stage and screen. He was best known for his portrayal of Dr. Watson in a series of films and in the radio series *The New Adventures of Sherlock Holmes* (starring Basil Rathbone as Sherlock Holmes). Bruce is also remembered for his roles in the Alfred Hitchcock films *Rebecca* and *Suspicion*. Bruce was the second son of Sir William Waller Bruce, 10th Baronet (1856–1912) and his wife Angelica (died 1917), daughter of General George Selby, Royal Artillery. Bruce was born in Ensenada, Baja California, Mexico while his parents were on holiday there. He was educated at the Grange, Stevenage and at Abingdon School, Oxfordshire. He served in France from 1914 as a lieutenant in the 10th Service Battalion-Somerset Light Infantry and the Honourable Artillery Company, but was severely wounded at Cambrai the following year, with eleven bullets in his left leg, and spent most of the remainder of the war in a wheelchair. He made his first appearance on stage on 12

I was waiting at the train station at Ford one morning to go to Bognor Regis. There was no one else on the platform except for an RAF regiment soldier. He asked where I was going, and I said, "To Bognor Regis." He said he was going there too, so we got on the train together. We got to talking, and he said, "I've never met anyone like you," and so forth. When we got there I tried to part ways, but he said, "When you're finished with your chores, will you meet me for tea?" So I said, "Oh, all right." We met at a nice tearoom, and he brought me flowers, but his table manners were appalling. He'd take a bite of toast and throw the rest on his plate. He was a thoroughly nice young man but rather uncouth. I asked what he did during peacetime. He said with great pride, "I'm a gravedigger." I said, "Oh, I'm sure you'll do very well." I was hoping he had a return ticket on the train and said, "I'm taking the bus back." He said, "Oh yes, I think I'll do that, too." So I had no choice. When we got back to Ford, he suddenly started talking about us getting married and having a little cottage. Good heavens, I was speechless.

When I went on night duty, with aircraft taking off on night sorties, we heard this noise coming from below the balcony. A controller sent our Cockney sergeant, Harry Greenbaum, out to investigate. He came back roaring with laughter saying, "There's some bloke out there with an accordion serenading Terry. You'd better go out and tell him this is an operational station." I went out, and sure enough there he was. I said, "Please go away." He said, "But I have to serenade you!" I said, "Well, do it some other time."

May 1920 at the Comedy Theatre as a footman in *Why Marry?* In October that year, he went to Canada as stage manager to Henry V. Esmond and Eva Moore and also playing "Montague Jordan" in *Eliza Comes to Stay*; upon returning to England, he toured in the same part. He appeared constantly on stage thereafter, and eight years later, also started working in silent films. In 1934, he moved to Hollywood, later setting up home at 701 North Alpine Drive, Beverly Hills. Nigel Bruce typically played buffoonish, fuzzy-minded gentlemen. During his film career, he worked in 78 films. Source: http://en.wikipedia.org/wiki/Nigel_Bruce

Finally, he went away, but I got teased a lot about "Gravedigger Dick." Fortunately, I never saw him again.

At one point in the control tower, we had a Canadian controller who was made the entertainment officer. He was very happy-go-lucky fellow. One night we were on night duty together, and he said, "I don't know anything about what the troops like to be entertained with, what films they like or these entertainment people who come in to perform for the troops. I don't know what they want at Ford Air Field. You're good at that sort of thing. You like the theater." I'm sorry I ever started that. So I said, "Yes, but what's that got to do with this?" He said, "Well, you know more about it. So you do this. You choose these people and the films and just sort of tick them off, and I will go ahead with it." So that's what I did. I tried to be conscientious when it came to the films by choosing films that I thought everybody would enjoy rather than just me, though I chose a little my way sometimes. Little did the station know that I was the unofficial entertainment officer for them, but I never heard any complaints.

We also had a very sweet girl who was a telephonist, who had the most beautiful speaking voice, which unfortunately did not match the rest of the package. She was a very short, dumpy person with hardly any figure and had a very pasty round face with stringy hair. Many pilots would telephone to speak to the controller about something or the other. They would hear her voice and fall over themselves to make a date to meet her with rather disastrous results. I felt so sorry for her because, you know, she just didn't match her beautiful voice.

Once one of the controllers decided he wanted to put a map on the wall using a straight ladder. He was a very heavy person. I don't know how much he weighed, but it was a lot. He was going to staple the maps on the walls. He covered a whole wall, and when he came to the last wall, what he asked me to do was to hold the ladder steady and to trap it with my feet under the bottom rung so it wouldn't shift. We did this successfully along most of the wall. When he came to the last part, he leaned over too far to staple one corner. When he came back, somehow his full weight was pushing inexorably the ladder down the wall, and there was nothing I could do to stop it. His sheer weight was pushing me back. I actually got some very bad bruises on the front of my ankles from trying to stop the ladder from coming back. It landed with a crash on the floor. He cut his chin open and had to have stitches put in. The next time we were on duty together, he said, "You know, every time I shave, for the rest of my life, I will be thinking of you." I said, "Not very kindly, I suppose." But there was nothing I could do about it.

I suggested he got permission to grow a little beard, like a Van Dyke, to cover up his scar; then he wouldn't have to shave there. Precedent had been set by an RAF officer who was a pilot in World War I and had been shot down. When he was in prison camp the guards there used a hot poker or stamp to press a shape of the German eagle on this man's chin. He was the only person in the RAF that was allowed to have this beard, which covered up this awful thing that had been done to him in World War I.

Chapter Twenty

END OF WAR, POW CARVER, ROAD TO BOGNOR REGIS, NORFOLK

I had been keeping up correspondence with Harold Carver, the American pilot of popcorn fame, who'd been shot down over Germany and was a prisoner of war in Stalag Luft 1. After his POW camp had been liberated by the Russians, I'd look out for the Dakotas that brought prisoners back to see if Harold might be on one of them, but he came in on another airfield. He called me up to tell me he was supposed to go straight back to the States, but he got permission to stay. He was up in London getting a new uniform and said he'd come down that day to check into to a hotel at Brighton. He said, "I dreamed all the time in the POW camp of sitting at the oyster bar and eating a dozen oysters. I'd love to see you."

I only had a few hours off because of the volume of air traffic we were handling, so I took the train into Brighton, and he met me at the station looking very thin.[1]

---

[1] Stalag Luft I was a German World War II prisoner-of-war camp near Barth, Western Pomerania, Germany, for captured Allied airmen. The presence of the prison camp is said to have shielded the town of Barth from Allied bombing. Approximately 9,000 airmen (7,588

I said, "How are you?" after all he'd been through. He said, "Fine, except for my feet." Harold's feet had either been burned or had frostbite, I forget which, and had never healed because he didn't get proper treatment for them in the POW camp. He said, "These new shoes are not helping the situation," as he had plaster and bandages on his feet. Walking down a hilly street, his new shoes slipped on the cobblestones. He didn't fall but he had to sort of stamp on his feet to recover his balance and said, "Oh, that's done it." We went to a chemist for bandages and salve. He asked me, "Would you mind changing these bandages for me?" "No, of course not," I said with trepidation as I could not stand the sight of blood.

We went back to his hotel and went into the bathroom. He put his feet in the bath to get the old bandages off. We soaked and dried his feet and redressed them. Bless his heart, I felt so sorry for him for what he must have been suffering in the POW camp. When we went downstairs past the front desk and out the door, Harold said, "You know what they're thinking." I said, "What do you mean, 'what they're thinking'?" He said, "That we were up to no good when we went upstairs." I said, "What? In the middle of the day?" It never occurred to me that there was more than one time of the day or night when you could have hanky-panky.

We went to the oyster bar. The server saw how pale Harold looked and said, "What have you been up to, chum?" I said, "He's been in a prisoner of war camp in Germany." Then everybody insisted on buying him drinks, and the oysters were on the house. Harold was

---

American and 1,351 British and Canadian) were imprisoned there when it was liberated on the night of 30 April 1945 by Russian troops. . . . The camp was opened in 1941 to hold British officers, but was closed in April 1942, when they were transferred to other camps. It was reopened in October 1942, when 200 RAF NCOs from Stalag Luft III were moved there. From 1943, American POWs were sent to the camp. Source: http://en.wikipedia.org/wiki/Stalag_Luft_I, accessed June 29, 2013

getting his just reward as best the British could do it. I had never eaten raw oysters. I tried one but couldn't swallow it, so I discreetly went to the ladies room, came back and ate something else.

Then we went along the waterfront and talked. He really didn't want to recount his experiences other than to say that when the POWs were released from the camp it was by Russians from Outer Mongolia who looked like savages who came clomping in with vodka. They sort of thrust the vodka at the prisoners with daggers in the other hand saying, "Drink!" The poor men had to drink this raw vodka and were violently ill afterwards.

When it was time for me to go back on duty, he asked me to marry him. I said, "Harold, I'm very fond of you but just as a friend. I'm sorry I can't reciprocate your feelings." I know he'd been thinking about that while he was a prisoner of war. He was disappointed, and if I had time I would have broken it more gently to him. We talked a little more, then he saw me back on the train. That's the last I saw of him. We did keep corresponding for quite a while after he got back to the states. His sister and I had been corresponding for a long time. She even sent me care packages. The first one included a pair of nylon stockings, which were absolutely unobtainable in England unless you knew an American. I dyed them grey and wore them for three years until they wore out. I guess the manufacturers realized they weren't making enough profit because the stocking back then lasted too long. Nowadays, they're made to last about one day.

When he flew home to Pasadena, California, he took aerial photos of the Rose Bowl and other well-known sites. I had never heard of the Rose Bowl. Every time I see the Rose Bowl parade now, I think somewhere out there is Harold with a family. It's rather nice to think about that. [See reunion with Harold, later on].

At night we turned off the runway lights until planes returned to the airfield. One night when the Mosquitoes were returning from a sortie, we had just turned the runway lights on when the duty pilot called out, "There are two men walking up the runway." The controller immediately told the pilot about to land to abort and go 'round again. He was just about to touch down, so he had to rev the engines and peel off.

The controller sent Harry Greenbaum out in the jeep to pick up these two men so the Mosquito could land. The two men were sailors who were terribly drunk. They came up reeling into the control tower and sort of blinked around. One of them said, "Where are we?" The controller said, "You are on a fully operational fighter station! What do you think you're doing, walking down the runway?" The man said, "Runway, mate? We thought it was the main road to Bognor Regis." Oh, dear. It could have been tragic, but was funny in retrospect.

Because of censorship, we didn't really hear that much about how things were going on the continent. The allies freed Paris and were heading east through the Low Countries [Belgium, the Netherlands, and Luxembourg] to Germany and Berlin. A friend of mine at Ford had a younger brother who was a 19-year-old paratrooper. They had landed a bridge they were supposed to hold and found themselves surrounded by Germans and taken prisoner. They had to march for days to a prison camp. It was such an appalling experience for this girl's brother that he completely lost every body hair. He had no eyebrows or eyelashes or hair left at all. He came home a broken man. It's sad to think about so many young people who were made old before their time.

As the war progressed and we got nearer to victory, our thoughts returned to civilian life, which almost seemed to be incomprehensible. It felt like we'd been at war forever. But I thought, *Oh I'm ready to be out of this uniform, go back to my art studies and pick up where I left off.* When D-Day finally happened, we were all exhilarated after six long years. The only fireworks we had were the rockets and flares we used for emergencies. The rockets were a bit dangerous because they had sticks attached, and when the rockets went off, the sticks would fall on the ground, so were bombarded with explosions of sticks like arrows.

Ford, 1945. Terry Smith (right) celebrating peace with controller and fellow watch-keepers.

I thought I would be out of the WAAF immediately, only to discover the WAAF was only demobbing [demobilization of armed forces] people according to one's age and not their length of service. I was seventeen when I volunteered and was twenty-two when the war was over. One of the watch-keeper girls, from Ireland was twenty-six and got out almost immediately. I thought, *Surely I'll get out soon because the Fleet Air Arm* [the branch of the British Royal Navy responsible for the operation of naval aircraft] *wants to take back their station again. I'll be redundant, so why can't I be released?* The CO, Tommy Thompson, said, "I want you and another girl to come up with me to open up a central flying establishment in Norfolk at West Raynham. It will be the first fully operational Gloster Meteor jet station. Maybe he balked my being released because I was experienced and he didn't want to train anyone else. But I thought, *I don't want to go to Norfolk. It's flat. It's cold. It's dreary.* I just wasn't interested even if it was the first jet station in the country. I just wanted get out of uniform.

The only experience I had with jets was a couple of years before when a jet was coming to land at our airfield. At that time, our jets could only stay in the air for 20 minutes. He came from another airfield and ran out of fuel on the downwind leg, but he was too high to land and went drifting on past us and ended up in a cabbage field. It should have been a very dramatic moment for us to witness this first jet landing, but all we saw in the distance was a car-rump and cabbages flying around.

So I wasn't too thrilled with the idea of going to Norfolk. He said, "Anyway, you need to have turnover time with the Fleet Air Arm staff in the Operations Room. You stay here while I make the arrangements. Rather mulishly I stayed on, and the Fleet Air Arm came in all spit-and-polish. Their first priority was to whitewash anything standing still. Posts were whitewashed. Chains were whitewashed. Buildings were whitewashed. It became a joke among those of us who were left that, "You better keep moving, or you'll find yourself whitewashed."

Whoever was on duty at 8 o'clock in the morning would announce over the Tannoy [public address system], "It is now 0800 hours." This alerts the station that it was the beginning of working hours. When they came, it changed to 0700 hours, and the controller informed me that I should say, "Wakey, wakey. Lash up and stow." I said, "Lash up and stow what?" The controller looked at me as if to say, 'What a question!' I said, "What are they supposed to lash up and stow." He said, "Their hammocks." I said, "You mean, the sailors on the station have hammocks?" He said, "Of course not. But it's tradition." Who was I to question tradition? So each morning, feeling rather foolish, I had to broadcast, "Wakey, wakey. Lash up and stow."

Eventually, my replacement took over, and Tommy Thompson said, "We're still not operational yet." I said, "Good lord, please let me out of the service." He said, "I've arranged for you to go up to Fighter Command Headquarters," at Stanmore in the north of London, "and tread water there until I can send for you." I was a little mollified because it wasn't nearer my parents' home. It was very boring because there wasn't much going on besides routine flights.

The operations room was underground on the estate of a baronet. One went through wrought iron gates, and on the left was a Georgian house, completely empty. There was a lake and quite extensive grounds. At the bottom of the grounds was where the Ops Room was located. I was in this glass booth. There was a young man next to me—I don't know what his function was—but we were talking one night, and he said, "You know, I'm a British Israelite." I said, "Oh really. I've never heard of them." He said, "We are the original lost tribe of Israel." He seemed so confident, who was I to argue with him. Then he said, "If you don't mind my saying so, I can tell you're one of us." I said, "Really?" He said, "Yes, I can tell that you are an original British and obviously then a member of the lost tribe and an Israelite!" I didn't tell him I had French and Irish blood and wasn't "pure" anything.

Eventually I learned they were now opening the airfield in Norfolk. Tommy Thompson came in a staff car and picked up the other girl and myself, and we drove up to West Raynham. I was miserable the whole time there. It was so cold and bleak. The war was over. I had joined to fight for my country. I had fought for my country the best way I knew how, and now I wanted out. I think I was there for another six months, but I was looking forward to not having to make that dreadful train journey down to London anymore. The trains were not heated, and in winter they were just freezing. As my circulation was not good, my extremities were blue by the time I arrived home. My dear father would bring me in the living room while Mother was making hot drinks for me. He would wrap warm towels around my feet, then he'd hold a foot between his hands to warm them up. To this day I'm touched that he was so sweet to me like that. I'd have a hot drink and couldn't wait to get into that beautiful, warm bath.

My military career ended with a whimper. The day I got my discharge papers, I had to have a letter concerning my performance while in the service. Tommy Thompson said, "I can give you glowing reports when you leave because you've done such a good job with me," but unfortunately he had to go away to some conference. The only other controller that had been there at Ford with me, a Canadian officer, had gone on leave, so they sent me to this WAAF admin officer, who didn't know what we Ops people did, to write out the report of my career whom I had never met before. She didn't know me. I didn't know her. She had no idea what I did in the service, and she said, "Well, what are you going to do now?" I said, "I imagine I will go back to art school and continue my career." All she wrote was "has interest in art," so I didn't go out with a bang. I left West Raynhan and the Woman's Auxiliary Air Force and didn't even have a party because there was no one there to party with. So I just toddled on home and faced life as a civilian. That was the end of my career in the WAAF.

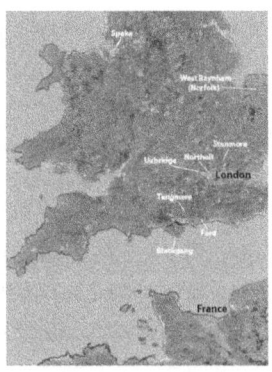

Locations of RAF stations where Terry Smith served as a member of the Women's Auxiliary Air Force during WWII.

HER FINEST HOUR

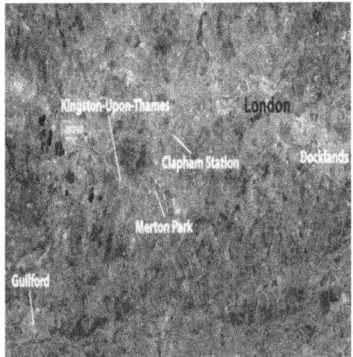

Locations of Terry-Smith homes (Merton Park, Guilford, Kingston-Upon-Thames) damaged by German bombs. Clapham Station is where a bomb landed just as Terry was getting off a train. Docklands is where her mother, Anne Smith, was directing relief efforts during intense bombing raids.

III. AFTER THE WAR

Chapter Twenty-One

RATIONING, RISE OF LABOR PARTY, CHURCHILL'S OUSTER

We knew little about my sister's, Sylvia's, escapades in Italy during the war. She was very good at languages and spoke Italian like a native. Being dark complexioned, she could be taken for an Italian. When she went to the officers' mess, the guard would try to turn her away until they got used to seeing her. They'd say, "Civilians aren't allowed in here." She'd reply, "I'm not Italian, I'm English!"

Sylvia was also in the room when General Clark accepted the formal capitulation from the Italians. She said, after it was over, reporters and others were grabbing souvenirs, but it never occurred to her to do that. She did liberate some skis from a mountain cave in northern Italy where there was a large cache of items stolen and hoarded by the Germans. They had cars, jewelry, art. Somebody said, "Would you like a Mercedes-Benz?" She said, "No, but I would like a pair of skis." She sent them home. My father and I picked them up at the train station. His car was small with a sunroof, so the best we could do was to stick them through it. Every time he went around a corner, they would slide side-to-side hitting either him or me.

They were so heavy, it was hard to control them. That's how Sylvia's career as a war correspondent and intelligence officer in the army came to an end. She left as a captain and I left as a technical sergeant.

So we were all back from the war and said, "We won the war!" Then we looked around and said, "Well, what exactly have we won?" Of course, we freed Europe from the yoke of Nazism and saved our country from being invaded by the Germans, but now what? We saw friends and relatives who had come back from the war shell-shocked, wounded, and some who did not come back at all. We looked around London filled with rubble still from buildings that had been bombed. No buildings had been painted since before the war. Everything looked grey and battered. No houses had been built since before the war and a great number had been bombed.

Lots of couples who had married during the war were coming back to find somewhere to live. They outnumbered the available homes. The government's answer was prefabricated houses, which were dreadful places, but they put roofs over people's heads. Companies started making utility furniture, which lived up to its name. A few years ago a public television station was auctioning "antique" English furniture. I had a good laugh when we saw it was utility furniture with masses of varnish being sold as antique furniture.

Couples who could afford to rent a flat [apartment] were gouged with exorbitant pricing, and the government clamped down by saying landlords could charge only a certain amount. The landlords got around that by charging a key fee. You had to pay a thousand pounds for a key to the flat. It was quite outrageous.

Everything was still being rationed. In fact, when I married in 1953, things were still being rationed. Food was rationed. Clothes were rationed. There was a long waiting list, sometimes two years, for new cars. Most people had taken their car wheels off during the war and had put the cars on bricks because of petrol rationing.

Then there was a shortage of tires when people started driving them again, even though petrol was still rationed. Cloth material was rationed. You had to decide whether to use coupons to make curtains or whether you'd rather have something to wear. Fine china and crystal was being exported. You had to get on a waiting list for those kinds of things. Young married couples had difficulty furnishing a house or buying essentials, and it was difficult finding good wedding gifts to give them.

People had to blame somebody for their situation, and a lot of them concluded it was the government's fault. When war broke out we had a conservative government, but during the war we had a coalition government composed of all of the parties—conservatives, socialists, and liberals. When we had our first election after the war, people voted heavily for the Labor Party. It was really outrageous how little the majority of the people understood the mechanics of government, the different parties, and voting. I volunteered to help at a local voting station and was astonished to encounter a very personable young man of about twenty-five who confessed he didn't know how to read or write. He had to put a cross by his name. I thought it fantastic [outrageous] that in 1946 anyone could get to the age of twenty-five and not be able to read or write. A lot of people didn't understand that the prime minister was determined by which party got in [power]. Many of them seemed to presume Winston Churchill would be prime minister regardless of which party won. Quite a lot were really upset that he was no longer prime minister. I remember reading that Churchill had been offered the Order of the Garter, a very high honor indeed, and he was quoted as saying rather bitterly, "As I've been given the order of the boot by my country, I feel I am not entitled to the Order of the Garter."[1]

---

[1] The Order of the Garter is the most senior and the oldest British Order of Chivalry and was founded by Edward III in 1348. The Order, consisting of the King and twenty-five knights, honours those who have held public office, who have contributed in a particular way to national

The Labor Party came in with great new projects. For instance, they guaranteed to take you from the cradle-to-the-grave. When you were born, that was paid for. Your schooling, medical bills, and college education was paid for. When you died, your funeral was paid for. Who was paying for this? The taxpayer. Poor, harassed doctors were being inundated for prescriptions for free aspirin and other medical items. It was a wonderful pie-in-the-sky idea, but having to pay wartime reparations and having so much money drained for the war, just 20 years after World War I, eventually broke down whole affair. Where there had been houses bombed in staunchly conservative districts, they put in flats for working class people who voted Labor. One would walk along the street expecting to see nothing but blue "Vote Conservative" cards in the windows, and suddenly you came across a plethora of red ones with "Vote Labor" on them.

There was mass emigration to Australia, New Zealand, and Canada for young people wanting a new and different kind of life after the war. The England the came back to was not the same England they were living in before the war began. Conversely, there was a mass immigration to England by members of the Commonwealth like India, Ceylon, Jamaica, and South Africa. All were welcomed to England as long as one member had a job waiting them when they got to England, then they could invite their families. Many of them invited their immediate family plus grandparents, uncles and aunts.

I'm afraid I'm painting a gloomy portrait of postwar England. But theatres, my first love, were opening up again. Pre-war, everyone wore evening dress when going to the theatre, but that

---

life or who have served the Sovereign personally. The patron saint of the Order is St George (patron saint of soldiers and also of England) and the spiritual home of the Order is St George's Chapel, Windsor. Source: http://www.royal.gov.uk/monarchUK/honours/Orderofthegarter/orderofthegarter.aspx, accessed July 4, 2013

changed when war broke out and nearly everyone was in uniform. After the war ended, the older generation wore evening dress, but the younger generation went in regular clothes, which was a good thing. But on the other hand, going out for an evening of dinner and theatre had once been a special occasion outside of everyday activities. If one just wore the same clothes, it was as if going to the theatre was like going to the grocers.

This was a whole new world and one very different from the one I grew up in during the 1930s. Every era has its great advantages and disadvantages, and we had to just go with the flow.

When Sylvia came home from Italy I said, "Oh, well, what are you going to do now?" She said, "The foreign office wants to send me to Vienna, but I told them, 'You promised me I could go to India after the war.'" I thought, *She wants to go to India rather than go to Vienna?* She was mad, and that was her future assured. But mine wasn't. I went back to the art school to interview with the head, Gerald Cooper. He said, "We're awfully short of models. Are you sure you wouldn't like to be a model?" I said, no. I felt quite insulted. "I want to continue with my art studies. Do you think I'm not talented enough?" He said, "No, no, it's not that at all. I'm just desperate for models for my live classes."

So I went back and studied theatrical design where you're drawing designs of sets and designs of costumes. But I found doing radar had made it impossible for me to concentrate. I was staring at the paper and not focusing on it at all and came to the conclusion that my career had gone down the tubes really truly and well. Having waited six years to get on with my art, it all collapsed. I thought, *Well, that's that. What am I going to do?*

Chapter Twenty-Two

HEATHROW CONTROL TOWER, CHARLES PERKINS

Living at home with my parents I did the usual things like Goodwood [horse racecourse], Henley Regatta, [Royal] Ascot [horse race], Chelsea Flower Show and exhibitions that were going on at that time. But I was just treading water. I couldn't decide what I would do, because apparently I wasn't trained to do anything. I would go and stay with friends. Then one day, a peculiar incident happened.

    I was going to visit some friends in the country, but I had to go up to Waterloo and get the underground to Paddington and then go down to where they lived. I can't remember where it was now, Wiltshire, I think. It was a dreary day, and I had to wait for my train. So I went to the waiting room, a big waiting room with a lot of people in there, and I sat down. I had a book with me and started to read. The man next to me started talking to me and, out of politeness, I answered him. He asked where I was going and so forth. Then he said, "I'm very interested in horoscopes, et cetera, and the stars. I think they influence us a lot. Now tell me when you were born and I can give you a horoscope." So I told him. When he started asking more probing questions, I realized I didn't want to talk to him anymore, so I got up and went out of the waiting room.

A man in a raincoat stopped me and said, "Excuse me. I'm a police officer in plain clothes. I was watching you talking to that man in the waiting room." And I said, "Well, he was talking to me rather." He asked me what we talked about, and I told him. I said I didn't like the trend of the conversation so I came out of the waiting room. He said, "We've been watching him for quite some time. They go after young ladies like you." I said, "Who go after them?" He said, "Well, I can't tell you." I said, "Are you talking about white slave traffic?" He said, "It's something like that."

When I reached my destination, my friends were there at the train station to greet me. When I got out of the carriage, they had to practically catch me because my legs were so wobbly. They said, "What's the matter? Are you not well?" I said, "No, I'm not ill. I just had a shock and a near escape. When I have had a cup of tea, I will be strong enough to tell you all about it." Anyway, that was my close shave, or brush with the white traffic gang.

When I got home, I really had to take myself in hand. I thought, *Well, I can't keep swanning around like a Sloan Street deb [area near Knightsbridge] without Big Daddy's money to support me.* So I had to come down to earth and think of something I could do to earn a living. My father was due to retire pretty soon, and I knew he and Mother would just be living on what he had saved over the years. They would be comfortably off, but they didn't reckon on having to support a grown daughter. I thought, *Is there anything that I've learned that I could use in civilian life?* I really couldn't think of anything until I thought, *I was in the control tower at the end of the war, so perhaps I could go work in the control tower in civilian life.*

I applied for a position at Heathrow's London Airport and went for an interview, which was a rather startling experience. I had to go up to the flying control operations room. Apparently unauthorized people had been wandering through the Ops Room and they had to turn people out. They had taken the knob off the handle of the door, and instead of that, they had sort of little opening like the old 1920s speakeasy where they would open a shutter and a face would appear.

So as I knocked on the door, the shutter opened. I had been exposed, as so many of us had, to servicemen who had been badly injured during the war. I remember going to dinner one night, and across from us sat a young couple. He was an air force pilot. They were a very attractive couple and were talking to each other. Then the waiter came up and spoke to them. The young man turned his head completely, and the whole other side of his face was just gone. It was very distressing to see that in a younger person. So when this shutter opened, there was this face, which was just a mask of different colored skin—purple, yellow, white. I just managed to control myself and say my name and "I've come for an interview." The door was opened by a charming man, Charles Perkins. I really don't remember the circumstances, but I think he said his cockpit had caught fire. His hands were badly burned. His face had no hair left. But when you got to know him, you completely forgot about his disfigurement. He couldn't even pick up a piece of paper. His fingers were sort of bent like claws, so he had to sort of scoop it up.

Some time later a new girl came to the control tower. One day we went for a cup of coffee, and she said, "Oh, isn't it terrible about Charles Perkins?" And he wasn't on duty at that time, so I said, "Why, what's happened to him?" She said, "His face." I said,

"Oh, that." Once one had gotten used to his strong personality, one didn't notice it.

I don't recall exactly what my job entailed—answering telephones as usual and getting sort of agitated with this glass ceiling that was still there. I said to one of the controllers, "When are they going to let women be controllers?" He looked at me astonished and shocked. "I can't imagine that would ever happen," he said. And then someone who was still in the WAAF told me that at last in operations they had made the Ops B; someone in the control tower who works with the controllers. Now women could apply. I had half a mind to rejoin the service and get a commission in Ops B. Then I thought, *Oh no, I don't want to wear a uniform again.* So I tossed that thought around for a few months while working in the control tower.

It's very funny really when you come to think of flying now and how everybody does. In those days, it was still a novelty. Heathrow Airport had a split flat roof for the control tower. On it was a man who used to give running commentaries to the public who paid so much to go up on top of the roof and watch the planes come in and out. Of course there were very few in that day; mostly cargo planes. It might be 20 minutes before the next plane appeared, so the commentary kept people occupied. But it was a rather annoying nuisance to hear this loud speaker above us announcing what planes were landing because we had to connect with them all the time to tell them what was coming in.

At that time our control tower was not far from the front gate. But when they put eight new runways in, they put the control tower in the center of it and knocked the old one down; enlarged the whole place. There was a little pub on the main road, which had once been a coaching inn. It was terribly old—I don't know, 14th century perhaps. That, too, was demolished to a certain extent.

STEPHEN DOSTER

But next door they had an airport hotel, which incorporated part of this very old building, so something was saved from it.[1]

---

1 In 1930, British aero engineer and aircraft builder Richard Fairey paid the Vicar of Harmondsworth £15,000 for a 150-acre plot to build a private airport to assemble and test aircraft. Complete with a single grass runway and a handful of hastily erected buildings, Fairey's Great West Aerodrome was the humble precursor to the world's busiest international airport, Heathrow. During World War II the government requisitioned land in and around the ancient agricultural village of Heath Row, including Fairey's Great West Aerodrome, to build RAF Heston, a base for long-range troop-carrying aircraft bound for the Far East. An RAF-type control tower was constructed and a 'Star of David' pattern of runways laid, the longest of which was 3,000 yards long and 100 yards wide. Work demolishing Heath Row and clearing land for the runways started in 1944. However, by the time the war had ended the RAF no longer needed another aerodrome and it was officially handed over to the Air Ministry as London's new civil airport on 1 January 1946. The first aircraft to take off from Heathrow was a converted Lancaster bomber called Starlight that flew to Buenos Aires. Source: http://www.heathrowairport.com/about-us/company-news-and-information/company-information/our-history, accessed April 24, 2013

Chapter Twenty-Three

BOAC, TRIAL FLIGHT, LOST!

I was getting used to seeing aircrew and flight attendants coming in from other parts of the world, talking about the wonderful food they had had and so forth. I thought, *Here we are in England. Everything is gray. No buildings have been painted or washed in the last years. The sun never seems to shine, and everything is gray and gloomy.* How I envied them and then I thought to myself, *Why don't I join the BOAC and become an air hostess?* Of course, it meant going back in uniform again, but at least I wasn't restricted in having to wear uniforms for eleven months and three weeks out of the year.

I went for my interview to the offices of the BOAC (British Overseas Airways Corporation) offices in Green Park, London and was ushered into a room with a row of formidable looking people sitting behind a table. One was a psychiatrist. I have no idea who the others were. I had to sit in a chair in front of them and be bombarded with questions. I just hoped I would muddle through it all right.

So I went to Aldermaston near Reading to start my six-month course. We learned first aid. That's another reason why I was accepted because I had done that sort of thing during the war. If somebody had a heart attack, we needed to know how to deal with that, et cetera. We had to learn how to mix drinks and so forth. About twenty or thirty stewards were taking the same course that we were. We would have exams every week on different subjects. We had to learn survival courses—jungle, desert, sea—any sort of situation that we might have if we force landed somewhere. We were shown how we would survive, and more important than us is how we would help the passengers to survive.[1]

One interesting moment was in the jungle survival course where we had to catch a crocodile, put a stick in its mouth, cut up its tail and make crocodile soup. We tried to keep a straight face while we were taking this course, but there were things that were too ridiculous. Another one was sea survival. We were taken out to the middle of a lake in a boat with a radio-signaling device, hoping someone would hear our appeal for help. I've forgotten how we were supposed to survive the desert.

We finally came to the day when we were going on a trial flight. Of the 14 other air hostess, or potential hostesses, I was the only one who had flown before. They were full of trepidation, which I thought it was rather foolish. Why didn't they take them up for a flight before they actually took the course in case they found

---

[1] RAF Aldermaston was a World War II airfield. It was used by the Royal Air Force and the United States Army Eighth and Ninth Air Force as a troop carrier (C-47) group base, and was assigned USAAF station No 467. . . . In 1947, the Ministry of Civil Aviation designated the airfield as a temporary civil airport and possibly a third London airport. In April improved facilities [were] installed when the training school was taken over by BOAC and British European Airways (BEA). On 30 September 1948 the school closed down. . . . The airfield was formally handed over by Air Ministry to the Ministry of Supply on 1 April 1950. There was in fact an unusual outburst of aerial activity on the day before the hand-over when, due to a slight misunderstanding at the Air Ministry, a number of pilots were given authority to land on the airfield for the purpose of conveying their clients to the races at Newbury. Therefore, 31 March 1950, marked the final day of Aldermaston's existence as an airfield. . . . The airfield site subsequently became the location of the Atomic Weapons Research Establishment (A.W.R.E.). The site dropped the A.W.R.E. name in favor of A.W.E. (Atomic Weapons Establishment) in 1987. Source: http://en.wikipedia.org/wiki/RAF_Aldermaston, June 2, 2013

they got airsick? Not for me to say. We went on this terribly noisy, converted Wellington bomber with no insulation. Because I had flown before, the radio operator handed me a flight book and logbook and asked me to keep a log of the trip. He would keep me informed about what we were doing.

We would be flying from Aldermaston to the west coast, across the Irish Sea to Ireland and back again. We were practicing looking after each other as we would if there were passengers. Periodically the radio operator would come back and say, "We're now at so-and-so degrees and flying at a so-and-so height and we're just crossing the Cornish coast." Then he came back a few minutes later and said to me, "Would you like to hear Princess Elizabeth and Prince Phillip exchanging their wedding vows?" I had completely forgotten. That's how excited I was about flying. I knew she was getting married, but I had forgotten that it was that day. It was the 20th of November, if I'm correct, in 1947. I went up to the cockpit, put on the headphones and, over the Irish Sea, listened. It was a most unusual way of hearing them exchange their vows. Then we turned around and came back across the coast again. By this time I had gone back to my seat.

The radio operator came back again and said, "Lend me your logbook a minute," and he wrote in big letters, "We are lost." I said, "What?" And he wrote, "Underneath, our instruments are gone," meaning they weren't working. He whispered to me, "We are flying blind." We certainly were in a dense fog. He said, "Don't tell the others." I said, "Of course not," because I thought they really would panic. Several of them had been airsick already and didn't know what to expect from one moment to the next. So we flew on. I was getting a little apprehensive myself. Suddenly we came out in to clear weather over land somewhere.

There was a railway handbook called a Bradshaw [railway timetable] where you could look up the times of any trains. He said,

"We're going back on the Bradshaw rail." I said, "What do you mean?" He said, "The captain has found a railway line. It's got to go somewhere." So we were just following the railway line until it came to a junction, then we followed that. By using the sun or whatever, we found our way back to Aldermaston. The rest of the girls never knew we were flying on a wing and a prayer at that moment. That was our first flight; quite memorable, too. Finally after six months, we had our final exams.

Apparently, I passed. I had to go to Great West London Road where the BOAC had its headquarters; a big building where they had all the uniforms. I had to be fitted for a uniform, then was told, "Now you will go down to the basement to pick out your wings." So I went down to the basement, to the counter and I said, "I've come to pick up my wings." The clerk showed me a table full of wings. I just picked one up and put it on. I thought, *Well, this wasn't much of a ceremony.* It meant I had passed. I discovered some years later, in America the airhostesses, I think they go on a dinner, their parents are invited and that is a great occasion. They go up on a platform and receive their wings. Oh, well, that's the English way, I suppose.

Chapter Twenty-Four

GAY PARIE, MAHARAJA OF GWALIOR, AUSTERE ENGLAND

I believe we had a couple of weeks off because I remember my birthday coming up. My sister was working for J. Walter Thompson, which, at that time, was the largest advertising company in the world. The main branch was in California, but she worked at the branch in Barclay Square in London. For my 24th birthday, she decided to take me over to Paris. Really nice. Looked forward to that.

So off we went to stay at a pensione [bed and breakfast]. The government wouldn't allow anyone to take more than 40 pounds out of the country. Part of the reason was that the labor party had promised that "we" would take citizens from the cradle to the grave, and any of our Commonwealth is welcome to come and join us. I call that 'the empire strikes back' because, boy, did we get a lot of Commonwealth—Pakistanis, Jamaicans, Indians, you name it. And, of course, we hadn't the funds so pay for all this, so the government implemented monetary restrictions. They didn't want it flowing out of the country. 40 pounds each was not a lot for two people. I was amazed when we went to Paris, considering it had been occupied by the Germans. It was as if there had never been a war; plenty of food. Nothing seemed to be rationed; although I'm sure there was rationing during the war. And here we were in England, after having won the war, still rationing in every way. We sort of looked on enviously.

We were walking one day down a very posh avenue looking at some boutiques along the way. In one shop there was just one garment in the window, which was a very fine display of blouse; very simple, black with Bishop sleeves. Sylvia said, "That would go perfectly with that black skirt that Mother lent you." I had only one dress in all of World War II, which I received for my 21st birthday. I didn't have anything to wear in the evening, so Mother lent me this long velvet skirt; but I still had nothing to wear on the top. I said to Sylvia, "This is a boutique. I know it's going to be terribly expensive and we don't have enough money." She said, "Well, I just remembered that I have business I do with an artist over here in Paris. J. Walter Thompson has opened an account for me there, so I will use the money in that account. Anyway, let's go in and try it on."

So I went in, not knowing whether it was going to be my size or not, and tried it on. Of course the sales clerk said, "None was there so fair. It fits you superbly; it could have been made for you. There's only one left; unique, exclusive." She went on so forth and so on. I was staggered at the price, but Sylvia said she would reimburse her company when she got to England. I was delighted with that!

A few days after we arrived, Sylvia read in the Paris papers that the Maharaja of Gwalior [India] was coming in to Paris to take part in the Le Grande Semaine, the polo week on the French coast at Deauville. They were friends of Sylvia's. At the end of the war, she was dying to go to India. She went there and worked for an Indian newspaper that was printed in English. She got to know the Maharaja through her work there, probably as an interviewer. When they arrived, she called them. They said, "Come and have dinner with us." So we went there that evening, but they didn't seem to eat until about 9 o'clock at night.

At the end of the meal, the Maharaja said, "Okay, I think it's time we toddle along to the Louvre, don't you?" I was sitting next to someone, I forget his name, and said, "Surely the Louvre is closed at this time of night." He looked down at me and said, "Not for the Maharaja."

We went along to the Louvre, and they had indeed opened it up just for the Maharaja. Money talks, doesn't it? It was really spectacular to have the museum to ourselves. Going up the stairs and seeing the Winged Victory [of Samothrace] statue lit up at the top of the stairs, we could really embrace the magnificence of it without other people milling around. The Maharaja was particularly interested in the Egyptian section, so we went with them. I pointed out a statue to Sylvia, and I said, "Doesn't his eyes look real?" And a voice said, "Mademoiselle, do not touch if you please." The whole group turned around and looked at me. I said, "Oh, dear, I was just pointing to it."

Anyway, they said the next day they were going up to Deauville and invited us to come along, and we said, "Well, you know, we're working girls. We have to get back to England in two days." They said, "Her Highness wants to return tomorrow because she wants to get to see some of the fashion in Paris," and so we agreed to go out with them. They had two Daimlers. We were in the first; the cook and the rest of his staff were in the second Daimler with the luggage. The horses had gone on ahead. The Maharaja and his entourage had flown to France on two Constellations, the largest airliner in the world at that time. One had the family, and the other had the staff and the polo ponies. We arrived there and stayed at Hotel Normandy, which was delightful. I ordered breakfast up to our room in the morning, and then, about ten o'clock, we went to walk around the corniche [waterfront]. Afterwards, we were going to have lunch with the Maharaja and some other people he had invited. Maharaja brought his chef from India, and we were going to eat Indian food. Sylvia loved Indian food, but I wasn't very keen on it; not having had much experience eating it except in Soho before the war. George said, "I was shaving this morning and saw you walking 'round the corniche." I said to Sylvia later, "Is it so unfashionable to be seen out before midday here?" I didn't quite know what the rules were.

So we sat around talking until 12 o'clock came and went . . . one o'clock came and went. I said to Sylvia, "I'm starving. If we don't go in soon, I'm going to have to go somewhere for a sandwich." Just then the manager came up and spoke to George Gwalior. He and another man got up and started to leave with their two wives, so we followed them. I think there was about ten of us. We wandered down a corridor, which had floor-to-ceiling mirrors. About halfway along, George stopped, looked at us and said, "I don't know what your plans are, but we are going to the men's room." So, rather red faced, we turned around and went back into the lounge again. At about two o'clock we finally did get lunch, which I didn't enjoy that much. I was so hungry I ate it anyway. That evening we went to a nearby casino and restaurant. The waitresses in the restaurant were students from the Sorbonne.

I think the whole place at Deauville was just open for this polo season; they were picking up mad money, I suppose. We repaired to have dinner there, I think about a half a dozen of us. We had been there a few minutes when the Argentine polo team came in and sat across the room from us with Aly Khan, son of the Aga Khan and the playboys of the western world. He had a black eye, and we wondered which irate husband gave it to him. I don't know if he was married to Rita Hayworth at that time, but I know he did marry her. She was one of his wives, although he only had one at a time. George said, "I can't stand that man." About ten minutes later, Aly Khan saw George and came across to speak to him. Of course they were slapping each other on the back like old friends. George started to introduce everybody around the table.

Incidentally, I was wearing this blouse that Sylvia bought for me in the boutique, and the only ornament I had on it was a diamond broach that Sylvia's husband, Angus, had given me when I was a bridesmaid at their wedding. Aly Khan working his way down after being introduced to various people at the table. Sylvia was sitting opposite me and she kept frowning at me; raising her head. I thought, *What's the matter? What is she trying to tell me?* I turned around to look, and right behind me was one of the waitresses. What was she wearing but a duplicate of the blouse that I was had on! It was so exclusive; only one of a kind! I crouched, wishing she would go away, but she just stood solidly there. When Aly Khan was introduced to me, I was crouching over the table and sort of waved feebly at him. He probably thought I was a hunchback. But I was very annoyed with my exclusive blouse that wasn't.

The next day we went back to Paris with the Maharani in the Daimler. Unfortunately, Sylvia got very seasick in the back of cars. Rather ignominiously, as the chauffeur was about to turn around in the median to park in front of the Hotel George V, Sylvia had to stop the car, get out and throw up—right opposite the hotel. They dropped the Maharani off, then the chauffeur drove us back to our humble little pensione. The next day the Maharani invited us to go around to some of the fashion houses with her.

They were putting on their fall collection. One girl was showing a three-piece outfit which had two jackets to go with a skirt and blouse, but she wasn't actually wearing a blouse. She calmly took off the one jacket to put on the other to display to us and was completely nude from the waist up, which was a little startling. But after all, this is Paris.

The next day we returned to austerity England. After years spent on air bases with rationing, it was somewhat of a shock going to France and seeing how the other half lived while we were with the Maharaja.

Ireland, incidentally, was neutral during the war and didn't suffer in the way of privations when it came to food and clothes. After we demobbed, I went there with an Irish friend, Carmel Baker, who was stationed at Ford in the control tower. Someone was getting married, so we stayed at Dún Laoghaire and went into Dublin quite a few times. It was the same in Paris. We were bowled over that just a few miles across the English Channel their lives were so different.

Chapter Twenty-Five

BOAC, EL ADEM, METAL FATIGUE

I had to report to BOAC headquarters for my assignment, which was Egypt—from London to Cairo. I thought it would be interesting. I had always been fascinated with Egypt and history. Another airhostess friend of mine was going across the Atlantic. She thought it would be fabulous because she would be able to buy nylon stockings and all the things we couldn't get in England. I thought that would be pretty boring because you just fly across the Atlantic and then come back again. But I would be seeing different countries en route to Cairo. I was told that I would have to have some shots, which I had to have every time I went overseas except America, and that on this first flight out I would be with another airhostess in order to assist her and learn the ropes. It was a tortuous route to Heathrow from Surbiton. I had to walk two blocks up to catch a trolley bus from Kingston on Thames. Then I had to catch a single bus from there to Hounslow, and then from Hounslow, I had to catch another bus out to Heathrow Airport. It took over an hour to do all that. When I arrived the traffic officer took me out to the aircraft. I got on and was introduced to the crew and cockpit crew. He says, "The other air hostess will come along shortly and take over."

Nothing happened. Then the passengers started coming on board, so I jumped into my role as the official air hostess, showed them to their seats, point out everything they needed to know and how to put on the seat belt, et cetera. Before long, the traffic officer handed me the ship's papers, and I said, "But where's the other airhostess?" He said, "She hasn't turned up. You're on your own, duck!" and he slammed the door shut. So as we were taxiing I had to demonstrate the life preserver, the Mae West as we called it, because we were flying over water at several stages. I put on a life jacket and demonstrated how to pull up the straps and how not to pull the cord, inflate the jacket, until you're getting out of the plane and so forth, but they must have given me an old model because the straps were rusted and I couldn't pull them up properly. I said, "Well, this is my old jacket. Yours is much easier to manage."

So we took off, but we had to keep landing all the time to refuel. We landed in France and then we landed in Rome, where we stayed overnight. I didn't serve any meals. I served coffee, tea and soft drinks. We would eat when we landed on the ground. We spent about two days in Rome, then we flew to Malta. From Malta we flew to refuel at El Adem in the North African desert, which is a little nerve-wracking because we flew over the area where my fiancé, Michael, had been killed.

El Adem was an oasis in the desert manned by prisoners of war left over from Rommel's army. As we flew over the coast of North Africa, we could see the trucks and tanks being covered by sand. It was rather unnerving being serviced by German prisoners of war; putting petrol into our planes. They hadn't been repatriated yet and were still wearing their German uniforms. This was in 1947, two years after the war.[1]

---

1 Gamal Abdul El Nasser Air Base is a Libyan Air Force (*Arabic*: القوات الجوية الليبية, Berber: Adwas Alibyan Ujnna) base, located about 16 km south of Tobruk. It is believed to have once had about 60 or 70 Mirage F.1EDs aircraft assigned. Prior to 31 March 1970 the airfield was

HER FINEST HOUR

On one of our flights, we had a layover for a week. One of the crew had been reading a book called *No Highway* by Nevil Shute about an airliner that flew for three years without incident. One day, the plane just fell out of the sky from "metal fatigue." We were flying over the Oman Peninsular later on and ran into a terrific storm with hailstones the size of golf balls. The plane was bouncing around all over the sky. There was a banquet sort of restroom in the back of the plane. I had taken a passenger's baby in a Moses basket there when suddenly the captain burst in and was trying to look around at the tail. In Nevil Shute's story the tail falls off. I said, "Did that book really get to you?" He said, "Yes. I've just seen if the tail's about to fall off." Years later, when the first jet airliner, the Comet, was flying from England, it flew for three years without incident and then crashed due to metal fatigue around the windows.

Airhostess Terry Smith at work.

---

known as Royal Air Force Station El Adem and used by the RAF primarily as a staging-post. Before the Second World War it had been an Italian Air Force airfield, and a number of the former Italian buildings were seen to remain in 2003 during a courtesy visit by former RAF personnel, at which time no military aircraft were in evidence. Royal Air Force Station El Adem was the fuel stop for the BOAC aircraft carrying the new Queen Elizabeth II on her flight from Entebbe to London on 7 February 1952. Source: http://en.wikipedia.org/wiki/Gamal_Abdul_El_Nasser_Air_Base, accessed April 28, 2013

At that time, our planes had curtains in the windows. This was before airlines used fire-retardant materials. On one flight, I believe it was to Johannesburg, a little man got out a little portable stove in the middle of the aisle and put a pan on it. He had a Sterno or some sort of flammable container and started to cook his meal. We might have picked him up at a stopover in Egypt. He didn't speak English and rather than eat our food, for religious reasons, he wanted to cook his own. I had to pantomime "No," but he insisted on cooking. Finally, the captain had to strong-arm him into his seat and put the flames out.

Either the Constellation or Argonaut, which I flew to Australia on one trip, had a combination lock on the cockpit door. Apparently someone tried to hijack a plane once, so they added locks for security; something I guess we got lax on again until 9/11. Each plane had a different combination lock number, which made it difficult to serve the crew if you forgot the combination. On another trip, an American family sat in the exit seats facing each other. The window was level with the wing, and their twelve-year-old son pulled the lever to open the window to see if it would work. It did. Immediately magazines were flying all about the place as the air rushed in. The window was pressed flat against the outside of the plane. I couldn't close it, but got one of the crew up front to close it.

Another time we were flying over the Mediterranean Sea from Malta to El Adem in North Africa. The radio officer opened the cockpit door and called me. He said, "We're going back to Malta," and pointed out his cockpit window. There was one propeller absolutely still. "We're only flying on one engine. Don't tell the passengers." So I went back and told them, "I'm so sorry. I know it's a nuisance, especially for those of you who have appointments in Cairo, but we have to return to Malta because we have technical problems that can only be dealt with there." El Adem was just a refueling station at that time. Of course, they all started grumbling, but I was praying no one would notice the dead engine. So things could get very interesting at times.

Airhostess Miss Marjorie Catherine Terry Smith, BOAC.

The stewards decided that we airhostesses were being treated differently, which we were because we had to have a certain standard of education, and the stewards didn't. Most of them had been waiters before joining BOAC. They said they took the same courses as we did, and we should all be called the same thing. The female of steward is stewardess. We airhostesses objected, but we didn't have a trade union, so they won, and we were called stewardesses after that. But then we started to be treated differently by the passengers; not that I was ever rudely treated. We didn't get the same respect as before, though. Passengers equated us with stewardesses on ships, who were maids. Later the airlines changed the terminology to flight attendants, which I suppose is better.

Our summer uniform was navy blue and khaki twill. We looked as if we were inmates of an orphanage. The Pan Am [Pan American] airhostesses wore these beautiful pale blue uniforms made of nylon. I once said to one of them, "We try to hide when you arrive because you look so glamorous in your uniforms compared to us."

She said, "We may look glamorous, but when we travel to humid countries the uniforms just stick to us and are very uncomfortable. Nylon doesn't breath." That was one good thing about our uniforms. We didn't feel hot in them.

I did enjoy seeing people in different nations still wearing their native clothes before the world attire became t-shirts and jeans. You're not sure which country you're in sometimes these days. On our stopovers, the crew would often go out and see the sights along with our passengers. You got to know the people you were flying with.

Chapter Twenty-Six

BOAC POSTER GIRL, BLACK HEAT, PROVING FLIGHT TO FAR EAST

Tip Pyle, the PRO [Press Relations Officer] at BOAC insisted on making me the poster girl of the airline. I told him, "Look Tip, I'm not the most photogenic or slimmest hostess in the BOAC. Please choose someone else." He said, "No, no, you're absolutely perfect for it." Bless his heart, he'd got a new thing for me. The BOAC had purchased 22 Argonaut Canadian planes that had only flown in cold climates and were going to be tested in the Near, Middle, and Far East. I was the "lucky girl" chosen for the maiden flight, which meant more training courses.

The first training was an introduction to this new oven that came with the Canadian plane. They called it black heat, which is what we know today at the microwave oven. We had to learn all the do's and don'ts, which was interesting because you were used to seeing flames or electric ovens with elements heating up. With this oven you saw nothing. We were told never to put anything with metal on it in the oven, nor plastic, a new thing that had just come out, because it would melt. The food came frozen

Terry Smith (right) with Tip Pyle (far right). Woman (center) from Kansas won a competition to name the movie The Accused. BOAC flew her to London as a prize. Terry showed her around London with Tip Pyle escorting.

Airhostesses Terry Smith, BOAC (left) and airhostess, Thelma Franco, Hong Kong Airways (right) at Great Ormand Street Hospital for Children.

in boxes. You'd put it in for so many seconds and it was cooked, which seemed like a miracle, and something we really needed on an airplane. They said not to let the package defrost in any way. At lunchtime, we served a meal cooked in the microwave. It looked absolutely delicious... very colorful... but when we went to eat it, it tasted nothing like normal food. We were told that's what happens when you don't put a frozen packet in the microwave. It would absorb the flavor of the cardboard box.

The day before our proving-flight/"Showing the Flag" trip, I got a call from one of the London daily reporters who wanted my bio. Then he asked me, off-the-cuff, about preparing for the flight, I told him about the jungle training. He said, "Are they serious about that?" I said, "I hope not." Then he said, "The things they expect you airhostesses to do!" The next day, the day we flew, we had all the dailies on board. I picked up that reporter's paper, which had an article about me. He twisted it around so that it looked like I said, "The things they expect us to do!" The whole thing was twisted around. I should have known, because years before the war, Sylvia had interviewed Charles Laughton, the actor. She sent him a draft of the interview for him to approve. He sent it back with a note saying, "You're the first journalist who ever quoted me correctly. Congratulations." She said she came to realize that on Fleet Street it's dog-eat-dog, and they embellish most everything written about anybody. So, take every interview you read with a pinch of salt. I should have learned from her to say, "No comment."

Our proving-flight captain, [A. P. W.] Crane, was a very formidable man who didn't approve of airhostesses at all. He was a no-nonsense, don't cross my path, sort of person. The last thing I wanted him to do was to read that article. I hid it away. It would be the *one* paper he asked for. I said, "I'm so sorry, sir. It seems to be the one paper we don't have onboard." He stomped away and said, "Well, bring me the *Times*." That was the beginning of our lovely journey.

We took off on the Argonaut Proving-Flight on June 13, 1949 with the BOAC chairman and all the board members to see us off. The name of the plane was *Ajax*. We were going to the Pacific and back—26,000 miles in 25 days. Onboard we had technicians and observers from the BOAC, the Ministry of Civilian Aviation, Canadian manufacturers, Rolls Royce, and Marconi. They took out some passenger seats and put two spare Rolls Royce engines there, which unbalanced the plane quite a bit, but that was the captain's problem, not mine, as long as we stayed upright.

The places we were scheduled to go to were France, Italy, Malta, Greece, Cyprus, Egypt, Palestine, Syria, Iran, Iraq, Pakistan, India, Ceylon [Sri Lanka], Singapore, Burma [Myanmar], Siam [Thailand], China, Hong Kong, Japan, and the Philippines.

Steward Cocklin was the chief steward, and he let me know it, too. The flight was pretty easy going as we were on routes I had been before. We ended up flying over Greece and over Cyprus without landing at either of those places. We didn't go to Palestine due to unrest or to China because they were closing their doors to foreigners for 30 years.

On the first day out, Stewart said, "We will serve consommé in the plastic cups, and we will warm them in the microwave." I said, "You can't put plastic in a microwave oven." He glared at me and put them into the microwave. Half a minute later he rapidly pulled them out, but they were all bent out of shape and had started to melt. He was furious with himself and more furious with me because I told him not to do it. I'm quite sure when we got back that he reported I had done it, because he was the sort of person. Then we had to serve everybody the best we could. So, I wasn't very popular with Stewart.

HER FINEST HOUR

When we got to Syria a reporter asked me if I was married. I said, "No, we airhostesses are all single. If we get married, we can't work for BOAC any longer." He wrote a headline that read, "Too Old For Marriage." The next day at the airport, the crew was going up the stairs and said to me, "Let us help you up the stairs, old dear. Perhaps you shouldn't be going up these stairs by yourself." They ribbed me for a long time about being too old for marriage. I gave up on reporters.

In Iraq or Iran, the mayor and a band saw us off. When they took the steps away, I went to close the door. Like in the war, when I was on that bomber, the door jammed against the plane and I couldn't close it. With a stiff smile on my face and waving to the dignitaries out there, they had to bring the stairs back and a mechanic had to pry the door loose.

One place that wasn't originally on the schedule was Kuwait, where it was absolutely burning when your feet touched the ground. There was nothing I could see on the skyline except for some camels. They interviewed us as we were standing in front of the plane, which was shimmering from the heat. I was standing in the front because I was the only girl there. I was sure that, like the Wicked Witch of the West, I'd be slowly melting into the ground if the interview went on much longer. Finally, we got into a coach [bus] and were taken to a hotel where the manager proudly announced that, "In six months we will have air conditioning!" I had a shower and lay down under the mosquito net. There was a ceiling fan that moved the air around a little.

When we landed in Hong Kong, the runway was facing toward the mainland with the mountains behind them. I had hardly stepped off the plane when the traffic officer said, "It will be very interesting to see you take off." I said, "Oh, in what way?" He said, "You're the first four-engine aircraft we've had here. Over there," he pointed to the distant mountains, "a two-engine plane crashed. And over there," he pointed to another place where a two-engine plane had crashed. "It will be interesting to see how you take off." I said, "I hope we can give you some entertainment." But I thought, *This is not a good omen.*

HER FINEST HOUR

Argonaut aircraft on 26,100 mile proving flight to Pacific

A 26,100 mile proving flight by one of our Canadairs—to be known as the 'Argonaut' class—began on June 14, when the airliner left London Airport on a twenty-five-days' journey to the Pacific and back. The aircraft, one of the first of the twenty-two Canadairs to be delivered, carried technical observers from the Corporation as well as from the Ministry of Civil Aviation, the Canadair manufacturers and the Rolls-Royce and Marconi firms.

Plans were made for it to fly an average of seven hours each day, interspersed with surveys and simulated instrument approaches at various aerodromes—apart from two days to be spent in Hong Kong, two in Tokyo and one in Karachi. The countries it was due to visit include France, Italy, Malta, Greece, Cyprus, Egypt, Palestine, Syria, Iraq, Iran, Pakistan, India, Ceylon, Singapore, Burma, Siam, China, Japan, and the Philippines.

The object of the flight is to give the aircraft—earlier models of which have already been well tried—an exacting test on the Corporation's routes, in changing climates, to finalise operational procedure in varied operating conditions and at many different airports before it is put into regular commercial service in the autumn.

It was arranged for landings to be made at twenty-eight different airports between London and Manila, in the Philippines, with simulated instrument approaches at a further fourteen airports, where the aircraft will not actually land. Although many of the airports included in the itinerary will not be regular stopping places for the scheduled services, the Corporation are satisfying themselves that diversionary airports are suitable for use by Canadairs.

The crew is as follows : Captain A. F. W. Cane, F/O. Capt. M. W. Raddon, Capt. C. N. Pelly, N/O. D. G. Dodson, N/O. J. D. S. Slater, R/O. C. B. Wilcockson, R/O. J. Walt, Steward J. Cocklin, Stewardess M. C. Terry-Smith, Superintendent Crew Capt. T. H. Farnsworth and Engineer Officer F. B. James. Also travelling on the aircraft as observers are : Capt. A. C. P. Johnstone (No. 1 Line), Mr. J. J. C. May (No. 1 Line), Mr. Morgan (No. 2 Line), O.E. Rudshaw (No. 1 Line), and Project Branch Representation.

Improvements to the York

No. 2 Line's maintenance staff at Hurn, under the Line Engineer, Mr. O. E. Chantler, recently modified twelve Yorks to reduce noise and increase their comfort and seating capacity.

The Yorks formerly carried eighteen passengers in two cabins, separated by a galley and toilets. This accommodation has now been moved forward, providing space for twenty-one passengers in one large cabin. Double-thickness windows and soundproofing materials in the cabin walls have made the aircraft much quieter than before. A false ceiling, concealed lighting and overhead racks have also been fitted, giving the cabin a more cosy appearance, and an aircraft conditioning plant has been installed in each aircraft.

The girl in the galley

The only girl in the Canadair party is Stewardess Marjorie Terry-Smith in the roomy and well-equipped galley

TOP PICTURE: *The Ajax at London Airport*

They had green Rolls Royces take us to the Peninsula Hotel. The end of the corridor overlooked the harbor, but there was a fire escape outside my bathroom. The day we were to leave, before daylight, I went to the bathroom to do my ablutions. Some workers were just outside on the fire escape smoking, and I daren't turn on the bathroom light. In those days it was very dry in the aircraft, and they didn't have moisturizing cream. I used Christy's lanolin cream in a blue-and-white tube. I also had toothpaste that was in a blue-and-white tube. In the half-light I managed to switch tubes. All of the sudden my face began to burn, and I ran into the bedroom to turn the light on. I had rubbed this darned Macleans toothpaste onto my face, and it was now fiery red. I had no choice but to go down to the crew bus. It wasn't until we were driving out to the airfield that the captain turned around and said, "Good heavens, what have you done to your face?" On a proving-flight where we were going to be interviewed wherever we landed, it was devastating. I said, "I hope it will wear off by the time we get to our next destination."

The other unscheduled stop was Okinawa, because we were short of fuel. We didn't have the correct means for paying for our fuel that the Americans wanted. They took us into this mess hall with long tables. About every five feet were masses of condiments, which were still rationed in England. "Oh, look, ketchup! What's that?" The Americans couldn't understand why we were so fascinated. They jokingly said, "If you can't pay for the fuel, we'll have to keep the stewardess as collateral. But we managed to negotiate payment.

When we got to Japan we stayed in Kyoto, outside of Tokyo. Tokyo reminded me of Manchester, England at the time. They had these overhead lines that trolley buses were attached to. Apparently they weren't used to seeing English people very much. When the crew and I stopped to look at things, clusters of people would eagerly surround us to find out our reactions to things we found interesting. They had a polite way of bowing to one another. We were walking down stairs at a department store, and there were two Japanese gentlemen ahead of us who bowed at the same time and bumped their heads. I don't know why I remember these little things.

I came back from the Kyoto hotel with two attractively covered menus, hand-painted every day. The artist got the equivalent of about ten cents for each one, I was told. I found Japan very interesting. I did see a few girls who looked very attractive in their native attire. Then there were Japanese girls, going around with American GIs, who dyed their hair blonde and wore short skirts. It just didn't look right to me.

Although I enjoyed going to all of those countries on the proving-flight, I was exhausted when we got home. The aircrew included two pilots, two navigators and two radio officers who could relieve one another while the others rested. However, there was only one airhostess serving the cabin the whole time. I was also apprehensive that the chairman of the BOAC would be at the London airport to strip me of my wings after reading that newspaper article. Fortunately, that didn't happen. But I did decide to resign at the time.

PROVEN ARGONAUT: The crew of "Ajax" soon after landing at London Airport from the proving flight to Tokyo. Left to right: Capt. M. W. Haddon, Nav. Off. J. D. S. Sloper, Capt. C. N. Pelley, Stewardess M. C. Terry-Smith, Nav. Off. D. G. Dodson, Capt. A. P. W. Crane (proving-flight captain), Capt. T. H. Farnsworth, Capt. J. C. Harrington (No. 1 Line manager), Eng. Off. F. B. Jones, Rad. Off. C. E. Wilcockson, Rad. Off. J. H. Lewis, Steward J. Cocklin. Also on the flight were Capt. Lilley, Canadair chief pilot, and technical observers from Rolls Royce, Marconi, B.O.A.C. Development Flight and Project Branch, and M.C.A.

Chapter Twenty-Seven

BBC, ANOTHER GLASS CEILING, TONY THE TIGER, GOOD OLD DAYS

I enjoyed my time at BOAC, but after two-and-a-half years, I didn't want to do that anymore. But what was I going to do? I was twenty-five at the time and didn't have a career. A friend of mine, Elizabeth Mellor, was working at the BBC and said, "Why don't you come and work here." I said, "What I'd really like to do is to get into television and do set or costume design." So I applied to the personnel manager. She said, "At the moment they don't have things organized to that extent at the television studio, but I will put your name down for that. In the meantime, would you consider doing anything else?" I said, "Yes, I have a friend at Broadcasting House in recorded programs. Is there anything in that line?" She said there was, so I applied and got a job working at Broadcasting House on the top of Regent Street in London.

I enjoyed the people working there, but it was a nothing job. I kept on applying for jobs that would help me get into television. The BBC was government run, and you got promoted on government levels, like G-1, G-2, G-3 and so on. When I applied for those different jobs, it turned out I couldn't jump all these numbers; I had to go through them. After two years, I went to the personnel manager and said I wasn't any nearer getting into television. She said, "Perhaps I should have told you that the trade union won't allow women into their union." I was so angry I resigned.

There again was that glass ceiling. I hope young people now working in anything they want to do realize how difficult it was for people of my generation. From the time I joined the WAAF, because you had to be aircrew to an officer in my field, then at BOAC and BBC, there were glass ceilings one couldn't rise above.

Meanwhile I had been keeping up my art by going to evening classes at a technical college on Regent Street. I met some people there who was doing the same thing. It turned out one was with Norman Hartnell, the Queen's dressmaker. His name was Colin McSweeney, an Irish marquis. Colin was completely zany. I enjoyed his company immensely. We had the same tastes in theatre and concerts. He was great fun to be with, but he got quite serious and eager to get married, but I still wasn't interested in anyone after Michael died.

I had a friend, Val [Valerie] Thomas, at the BBC who was a born leader. She got us all to go to lunchtime services at the Regency Church, a stone's throw from the BBC. Her mother had a chain of cinemas across some part of England, but she never came up to London. Val would get passes for cinema owners and critics to view movies before they were presented to the public. She would ask me to go with her at ten o'clock in the morning to see the latest film to be offered to the public. She would say, "I have no idea about this movie. What do you think?" I'd say, "I think it's one the general public would like." So I was back again doing what I did in the WAAF for that entertainment officer; giving my opinion on which films her mother should choose to put in her cinemas.

While I was at BBC, Sylvia was also working as a copywriter

in Barclay Square with J. Walter Thompson, one of the biggest advertising firms in the world. She and many of the other copywriters were really writers. They got such fabulous salaries that they earned enough to take a year off and write a book. Sylvia wanted to go to Afghanistan for a year with a French archaeology group to unearth a palace, but she needed the money first, so she was working for J. Walter Thompson, which had the accounts of Proctor & Gamble and Kellogg's. Someone in J. Walter Thompson's advertising agency had crated this tiger for their new Frosted Flakes, but they didn't have a slogan for it, so they put it out for anybody in the organization to come up with one. Sylvia was dating someone named Tony at the time, and she came up with the slogan, "Tony the Tiger says 'They're G-r-r-r-eat!'" Apparently, Tony the Tiger and his slogan are still going strong.

Sylvia and I shared an apartment in a block of Regency houses at the top of the road between BBC and Park Crescent. A lot of the houses were formerly owned by the aristocracy but were now homes to foreign embassies. I found it fascinating going to work each morning and passing by them. At that time they wore the native costumes of Burma, Syria, Cyprus, or wherever. I chatted with them and got to know some of them quite well. That's why I was always the last one to get up to Recorded Programming. The others came in from Surrey and other places on the trains. I only had a ten-minute walk but got delayed talking to people.

We lived on the ground floor of a townhouse. Our landlord used to rent out the front porch for photoshoots of models. The bend in the crescent shape the row of these townhouses formed made an attractive backdrop. One always had to be careful going out the front door that you didn't have a model fall in on you or that you didn't get tangled up in the trail of wires leading to big lamps.

Townhouse crescent, London.

Looking back, I realized I took it for granted that every week we went to a new play or concert or art exhibition. I thoroughly enjoyed the merry-go-round of living in London. It's only afterwards that I look back nostalgically and think those were the good old days.

DENOUEMENT

Terry was reunited with Harold Carver in 2012:

"In 2011, 66 years after the war ended, my grandson, George Dorrance, was interested in my war experiences. I had photos of Harold, and George asked me about him. I said, 'I knew his family lived in Pasadena, California, but I don't know what had happened to him. We wrote for a while but we lost touch.'

George somehow managed to locate Harold's telephone number on the Internet, and lo and behold, about a week later, he called me up on the telephone, someone I hadn't heard from for nearly 70 years. It was quite amazing to get in touch with him. He's now 96. It's amazing that we could get talking again about reminiscing and things from his point of view and from my point of view. My goodness, what a reunion! In 2012 our children managed to bring us together at his daughter's home in Virginia.

Terry and Harold Carver, 2012

THE TERRY-SMITH FAMILY

Terry's father, William Horace Smith, passed away in 1962. Her mother, Anne, outlived many of her doctors and died at the age of 106. Terry's sister, Sylvia, went on to write mystery novels using the pseudonym Max Munday. Her memoir, *The Tigers of Baluchistan* (Sylvia Matheson), details her experiences living with Bugti tribesmen in Baluchistan who made her an honorary tribal chief. Her books, *Time Off To Dig: Archaeology and Adventure in Remote Afghanistan* and *Persia: An Archaeological Guide*, were well-read archaeological resources and are still available via online booksellers. She later became a fellow with the Royal Geographical Society. Sylvia served as a tour guide in her beloved India and wrote text for *Rajasthan: Land of Kings* (photography by Roloff Beny). She and her second husband, Henry Schofield, were forced to leave their home and possessions in Tehran during the 1979 Revolution. They eventually settled in Javea, Spain, where she continued her literary and archaeological pursuits. Sylvia passed away in 2006. More details about her life can be viewed at the following web sites.

The Daily Telegraph:
http://www.telegraph.co.uk/news/obituaries/1514823/
   Sylvia-Schofield.html
Encyclopedia Iranica:
http://www.iranicaonline.org/articles/
   matheson-sylvia-writer-traveler-archeologist

Sylvia in Baluchistan.

TERRY SMITH

After her time working for the BBC, Terry Smith traveled to the United States aboard the Queen Mary. She would return to London where she met George Doster, an American Naval officer who had served in the Pacific aboard the *USS Taylor*, the first destroyer to anchor in Japanese coastal waters at the end of World War II. They would eventually marry and settle on St. Simons Island, Georgia, his home state, where they raised five children: Sarah, Jonathan, Nicholas, Stephen, and Charlotte. Terry still lives on St. Simons. On August 13, 2013, she celebrated her 90th birthday.

Terry Smith (center) about to board the Queen Mary. Sylvia (left), Anne Terry-Smith.

Terry arriving in New York harbor aboard the Queen Mary.

George Doster

Terry's children (L-R: Jonathan, Charlotte, Nicholas, Stephen, Sarah).

Terry on her 90th birthday presenting the "queenly" wave.

Terry, surrounded by her grandchildren on her 90th birthday (L-R: Ellen, Stephen, George, Sarah, Andrew, Emily)

90th Birthday card by George Dorrance.

ABOUT THE AUTHOR

Writer and oral historian Stephen Doster was born in Kingston-on-Thames, England, and raised on St. Simons Island, Georgia. He is the author of both fiction and nonfiction, including two oral histories. Doster's literary works are focused on Georgia and its coast. He holds degrees from the University of Georgia and Vanderbilt University and currently resides in Nashville, Tennessee, with his wife, Anne.

STEPHEN DOSTER

FROM OPEN ROAD MEDIA

INTEGRATED MEDIA

Find a full list of our authors and titles at www.openroadmedia.com

FOLLOW US
@OpenRoadMedia

www.ingramcontent.com/pod-product-compliance
Lightning Source LLC
Chambersburg PA
CBHW032224080426
42735CB00008B/707